Embrace the Chaos, Enjoy the Journey
A Leadership Path for Students and Young Adults

Embrace the Chaos, Enjoy the Journey is a great call to action for youth to actively pursue leadership in their personal and professional lives. As Bill McKenzie describes, our current social reality is characterized by chaos and unpredictability. His new book provides an efficient guide of how young people can wisely navigate this chaos and break down community barriers. McKenzie's advice will set up students to persevere as leaders while having the power to change society for the better!
 —Kazara Williams, Undergraduate Senior at UNC-Chapel Hill, a Johnston Scholar

This invaluable work is a must read for all young adults! Readers will receive vital leadership information, information that will enhance their quality of life and that of their communities. Bill McKenzie's book will remain one of my most treasured possessions.
 —Captain Francena Walker, US Army

This book is the leadership book of all time! It is most definitely a must read for all high school students, especially seniors. The leadership qualities discussed in this book will help you become a successful person in whatever you do. What an awesome book!
 —Billy Hawkins III, recent college graduate

As an outdoor professional working with young adults for over twenty years in adventure education, I am always looking for resources that provoke a forward-thinking agenda for my staff and program participants. Bill McKenzie's *Embrace the Chaos, Enjoy the Journey* gives me the tools to assist young adults in making positive life changes.

—**Andrea Galioto-Evans, YMCA camp professional**

Bill McKenzie brings leadership to life for students by addressing them from the perspective of a college athlete, CEO, triathlete, and father. The outcome is a leader's handbook: an insightful, practical, and uniquely personal resource that engages the leadership potential in all of us!

—**Ashlie Bucy, marketing executive**

Just finished it and really enjoyed it and it speaks to many audiences. Within the army specifically, I'd see utility in leadership training. We could use it in our own training in my brigade. I am sending it to my freshman in college for her use!

—**Lt. Col. Michael Faruqui, US Army**

Leadership comes naturally to some. The rest of us need help learning how to lead, and the earlier the better. Bill McKenzie's new book, *Embrace the Chaos, Enjoy the Journey*, will provide young adults with a good place to start. The timing couldn't be better for needed leadership.

—**Jack Dillard, Marketing Consultant**

Insightful and inspirational, Bill McKenzie paints a portrait of what a good leader should be, in a way that is practical and easy to apply.

—**Gavin Andrews, recent college graduate**

Bill McKenzie's insight on leadership is eye-opening. His new book, *Embrace the Chaos, Enjoy the Journey*, is full of great leadership examples and I enjoyed reading his thoughts on this critical and timely subject!

—Latoya Bullock, Vice President of Community Impact, United Way of Greater High Point

Bill McKenzie has given me a valuable blueprint for what a successful leader should look like!

—Bryan Soltis, recent college graduate

Bill McKenzie's new book is timely and powerful. I would recommend this book to every young adult today, regardless of career path desired. I am recommending it as a mandatory read for my fellow soldiers!

—Sgt. 1st Class James A. Leuvano, US Army

I found Bill McKenzie's book to be an amazingly clear and to-the-point assessment of authentic leadership. It's a topic rarely discussed outside the corporate tower, but one all young adults absolutely must embrace. I now feel better prepared to maximize my college education and career beyond!

—Tory Bowers, recent college graduate

Our secondary school used Bill McKenzie's first book for a "lunch-and-learn" for our graduating students and the reception was amazing! His new book, *Embrace the Chaos, Enjoy the Journey* should be required reading, not just for students, but for their parents as well.

—Carol Widmeyer, MSLS, school guidance and media specialist

Embrace the Chaos, Enjoy the Journey, is an exceptional read on leadership. The chapter on female leadership especially spoke to me as a woman in former leadership positions. I wish Mr. McKenzie's book, and especially the chapter on women's leadership, had been written before I began my professional career. I enthusiastically recommend this book to all young adults. It can make such a difference in beginning your professional career!

—Georgiana Gekas Wellford, JD, University of Richmond

This week, as I was completing recommendations for students applying to The Governor's School of North Carolina, it occurred to me that each student who will attend this prestigious program should read *Embrace the Chaos, Enjoy the Journey* by Bill McKenzie. I think this book is a "life map" for students and young adults who will be our leaders of the future. *Embrace the Chaos* is a must read for all of us!

—Barbara M. Carter, MEd, secondary school math teacher

Bill McKenzie continues to challenge people to be better. To say a young person (or really anyone) needs to read this book is an understatement. If someone wants to know how to be prepared for their future in this chaotic world, Bill's book will give them insight into the challenges they will face and how best to find success. As a YMCA executive, I have worked with hundreds of teenagers and young adults and I have seen the "lights come on" after they have read Bill's books. Read *Embrace the Chaos, Enjoy the Journey*. You will be inspired, challenged, motivated, and prepared for wherever life takes you.

—Michaux Crocker, executive director, YMCA camp Cheerio

There is such a great need for outstanding leadership in today's chaotic and uncertain world. Bill McKenzie challenges and inspires young men and women to take the path less traveled, to pursue a life as a servant leader, to go where many will not, and to show strength, decency and compassion on their leadership journey. *Embrace the Chaos, Enjoy the Journey* offers that path forward!

—Ashby Cook, Midtown Financial, financial advisor

Having been a college basketball coach my entire life, I have always been interested in effective leadership. Having researched and read numerous articles and books on the subject, I know that leadership is a learned trait. Bill McKenzie's *Embrace the Chaos, Enjoy the Journey* is a remarkable book. I guarantee you will enjoy and profit from reading it!

—Butch Estes, head basketball coach, Barry University, Miami, Florida

Wow! What a fantastic leadership book! As a young female entrepreneur, registered dietitian, marathon runner and coach while I work to build an online business, I found the chapter on Women Leaders Rising to be both exciting and motivational. We live in a society that should have more women leaders and I am facing some of those challenges daily. I have no doubt that Bill McKenzie's *Embrace the Chaos, Enjoy the Journey* will be a life-changing read for many young people who aspire to become effective leaders in both life and business. This is a MUST read for all young adults!

—Kayla Slater, MS, RD, CDN, founder of Plant-Based Performance Nutrition and Run Coaching, LLC

Bill McKenzie's book, *Embrace the Chaos, Enjoy the Journey,* should be available in all of our schools! It addresses what is happening in our nation today and is a GREAT guide to what students and young adults need to know about serious leadership. As a community volunteer, business owner, parent, and past school board member, I speak to young people all the time. I know the importance and value of effective leadership, and *Embrace the Chaos*, simply put, gets to the bottom line!

—Ed Price, Guilford County North Carolina School Board Member, 2010–2016

As a retired Middle School teacher, I can emphatically applaud Bill McKenzie's new book, *Embrace the Chaos, Enjoy the Journey*! I only wish this book had been available to me when I had classrooms of eager students. They would have been inspired by Bill's discussions of perseverance and teamwork and the critical importance of becoming a serious leader. Every classroom teacher in our country would benefit owning a copy!

—Charlotte Amos, Middle School teacher

Embrace the Chaos, Enjoy the Journey should be the basis for classes and lectures for both high school and college students. Bill McKenzie's chapter on 'Creative Disruption' is timeless. I love the encouragement this chapter offers to stir up change. My children are in college and this book addresses what they are facing today and tomorrow – a world that is constantly changing and one requiring them to thrive as they navigate complexity and volatility. This book is a great study on a critical topic – leadership!

—LaTrinda Moore, Parent and Entrepreneur

Extraordinary results require extraordinary decisions. Extraordinary decisions often require a large measure of risk. Risk requires a high degree of comfort in areas of discomfort. Welcome to the zone high-impact leaders revel in.

Embrace the chaos and enjoy the journey.

EMBRACE THE CHAOS,
ENJOY THE JOURNEY

WILLIAM R. MCKENZIE, JR.

EMBRACE
THE CHAOS,
ENJOY
THE JOURNEY

A LEADERSHIP AWAKENING
FOR STUDENTS AND YOUNG ADULTS

Charleston, SC
www.PalmettoPublishing.com

Embrace The Chaos, Enjoy The Journey
Copyright © 2021 by William R. McKenzie, Jr.

Paperback ISBN: 978-1-63837-517-3

This book is dedicated to all US military personnel and their families and to all the health care personnel and first responders working during the coronavirus pandemic and beyond. Your sacrifice is unquestioned and your leadership is beyond measure. The example you provide is both extraordinary and humbling.

Thank You

Chaos gives birth to dancing stars.
—Friedrich Nietzsche

The future of work is skills, so stop worrying about degrees.
—Jamie Dimon, Chairman/CEO, JP Morgan Chase

CONTENTS

CONTENTS

INTRODUCTION

To say that today's world is chaotic is the ultimate understatement. To realize that there is a serious leadership deficit across the globe is a close second.

It's often said that the subject of leadership is the most overly analyzed, overly examined, and overly discussed topic in the business world. I will argue that it is *the* most critical subject of our time, inside or outside, of our business environment.

This book is about effective and meaningful leadership for students and young adults. In the following pages you will *not* see an intellectual treatise on this subject nor will you read a Yale Business School case study of the topic. That is not my intent. What you will see is a concise overview of select key leadership attributes, behaviors, and challenges that every young person should embrace and relentlessly commit to.

This book has a singular focus, and that is to make young adults aware of how critically important authentic leadership is to their personal happiness and success as they navigate a chaotic and disruptive world. There are certainly many more leadership attributes to recognize beyond the ones outlined here. However, I have chosen a short, select list of those attributes, behaviors and challenges that can, and will, change a young life.

Leadership is not a spectator sport. No one has the luxury today of sitting on the sidelines and watching, assuming that somehow their lives will get better if they can just weather the storm. Yet, research tells us that is exactly what so many people are doing today. A majority of Americans look for structure and predictability in their lives. They don't want to be talked about, don't want to be ridiculed, and work very hard at "fitting in." They search for that all-important comfort zone and have little desire to move out of it. They may not like the status quo but, despite paying lip service to the contrary, they stay put.

We don't plan to fail—we just fail to plan. This becomes a cult of average. This is not leadership.

We can do better. We must do better.

Leaders of the future will be challenged not with expected problems, but rather will face a world full of "dilemmas." This will require a new way of thinking, a need to move into areas of some discomfort, a willingness to take great risks, and a move from just being smart to becoming truly wise. New leaders will focus on elevating their teams with more humility and kindness and move away from the macho bravado model so often in play today (and yesterday).

Acquisition and consumption are dominating the chaotic business world. Contemplative leadership, marked by prolonged thought and reflection, will get serious attention, as will the recognition of the power of "decent" leadership. The term "servant" leadership will also become a strong motivator in much of what future leaders will add to the greater humanity.

In many respects, leadership is common sense but not common practice and make no mistake, we have a serious leadership deficit today. As business author Jeffrey Krames writes in his 2015 book *Lead with Humility: 12 Leadership Lessons from Pope Francis,* "We live in an age marred by a dearth of leadership. Today, fewer leaders roam the halls of our largest corporations, setting examples of positive, effective leadership."

We also know that scarcity creates value. For those who commit to a life of brave, courageous, and effective leadership, those who are willing to move into areas of extraordinary uneasiness and chaos, the personal returns and expanded impact will be significant. And yes, your leadership journey will be filled with highs and lows, but the highs will exceed the lows if you stay brave and committed.

The leadership world is truly one of great challenge, excitement, and personal discovery. This little book can help that journey, so read carefully, read joyfully, read thoughtfully, and strive to create meaningful change for yourself and others along the way. You'll be glad you did, and collectively, our world will thank you.

So, be prepared to embrace the chaos! Enjoy the journey!

A WORD TO STUDENTS

There must be some kind of way out of here, said the Joker to the Thief, there's too much confusion, I can't get no relief.
—Bob Dylan/Jimi Hendrix, *All Along the Watchtower*

Let me begin this book with a very simple sports analogy.

You can't play professional sports without mastering the fundamentals.

The same holds true with leadership. If you want to become a leader with vision, inspiration, motivation, empathy, accomplishment, and the ability to create thoughtful and meaningful change, you will need to commit to the very basics of effective leadership—the key word being "commit."

That's what this book is about.

If you didn't read the introduction, please do so now. I'll wait. Here's the deal.

A lot of stuff is important in life, but at least two things are really important: your happiness and your success, and that's what leadership is ultimately about.

The potential consequences of reading this book are high impact. They're exciting, they're about taking charge, they're about making good things happen, they're about your ability to create profound change, they're about becoming a catalyst, and they're

4

about realizing a life of happiness and personal success, even in a seemingly never-ending tsunami of daily chaos and complexity.

I'm sure you know there's a lot of disruptive noise in the world today and I don't use the word chaos lightly. It would seem that the only *certain* thing in the world today is its *uncertainty*.

Your challenge, every effective leader's challenge, is to learn how to navigate and embrace a chaotic world, a world often thought to be upside down, and to find a meaningful measure of personal success and happiness. You'll want to move away from the constant distractions that clutter daily life. Move away from "bad air," eliminate "loser talk," and look to be "productively disruptive."

Don't confuse this daily noise with substance and challenge. You, no doubt, are aware of some of the incredible challenges and opportunities you face today. Here are just a few that will require your attention and leadership:

➤ It's estimated that the average person today clicks, swipes, or types a reported 2,600 times a day on their smartphones, as college administrators continue to report a lack of conversational depth among young adults.

➤ The 2020–21 COVID-19 pandemic will cause 34 percent of millennials and 26 percent of all workers to look for a new job.

➤ 2.2 million people are in jail on any given day in the US, while a reported 20 percent of Americans have a criminal record of some kind.

➤ In 2018, a typical American family with health insurance spent more than $12,000 on health care premiums, deductibles, co-pays, and uncovered costs, and an estimated 40 million people chose not to see a doctor because of those costs.

➤ A 2020 Centers for Disease Control and Prevention study found that the age group eighteen to twenty-four reported experiencing at least one behavioral or mental health symptom as the COVID-19 pandemic caused unprecedented health and societal challenges.

➤ The world now has more people over the age of sixty-five than under the age of five, and that ratio is growing; this could present obstacles to economic growth.

➤ A 2019 *New York Times* survey found that 74 percent of parents admit that they have made appointments for their eighteen to twenty-eight-year-old children, 16 percent helped write their job or intern application, and 11 percent called their child's employer when an issue arose.

➤ Amid the 2020–21 COVID-19 pandemic, a reported 52 percent of US adults ages eighteen to twenty-nine moved home to live with their parents as jobs were lost and colleges and universities were closing on-campus classes.

➤ In 2018, the poorest half of American families had an effective tax rate of 24 percent while the wealthiest 400 households paid a rate of 23 percent.

➤ Middle class wages are relatively stagnant while CEOs of the largest US firms earn an average of $15 million per year, almost 300 times more than typical workers.

➤ Female founded companies received less than 10 percent of venture capital deals in 2017, yet companies with female board members and female senior executives consistently outperform many companies dominated by male executives.

➤ Next to China, the US is the largest emitter of greenhouse gases in the world.

➤ Sea levels are expected to rise by more than three feet by 2100, inundating many coastal communities; Greenland is losing 300 tons of glacial ice a year.

➤ An estimated 25–40 percent of young people are simply too heavy to enlist in the military.

➤ Student college and university debt has reached $1.5 trillion, placing serious stress on both students and the US economy.

➤ 43 percent is the percentage of college graduates whose first jobs do not typically require a college degree.

➤ In 2019–20, only 7 percent of public school teachers in the US were Black, according to the Stanford Graduate School of Education and the National Center for Teacher Residencies.

➢ Less than 2 percent of the US population provides the nation with safe and affordable food.

➢ A 2018 North Carolina works commission found that 67.3 percent of employers looking to hire cited employ-ability as a challenge: a lack of soft skills such as com-munication, teamwork, critical thinking, and creativity.

➢ One in six families suffer from food insecurity in the US, and almost 20 percent of children live below the poverty line. Child poverty costs the US an estimated $1 trillion annually.

➢ In 2020, scientists reported that 1 percent of the world is a barely livable "hot zone" and by 2070 that portion could rise to 19 percent, leading to a massive climate-driven migration from Africa, Central America, India, and Southeast Asia.

We live in a cacophonous age, swarming insects of noise and interruption buzzing about—emails, text messages, wireless web connections, cable news, cell phones, meetings, social media posts, and all the new intrusions invented by the time you are reading this. If leadership begins not with what you do but with who you are, then when and how do you escape the noise to find your purpose and summon the strength to pursue it?
—Jim Collins, author of *Good to Great*

Many of you are now experiencing what might be called a *technology paradox*. The more technology you acquire, the less productive you become. You may be focusing on "news you can't use." As detailed in the provocative neuroscience book *The Shallows*, your brain may become rewired, and your focus drifts away from necessary and useful information; rather, it often migrates to the unimportant, the useless, and the ridiculous. A Kent State University study found that students who were heavy cellphone users tended to be more anxious and have lower grade point averages. The study also revealed that students said they felt a real sense of obligation to stay constantly connected through their phone. This never-ending connectivity led to a significant source of stress for students surveyed.

If this is you, let me encourage you to drop the attraction-for-distraction agenda, get a serious grip, and move in more meaningful circles of information. You cannot, nor will not, become an effective leader if the gravitational pull to your cell phone is overwhelming.

Recent data coming out of education at the college level is horrifying. One reputable survey found that 36 percent of students demonstrated no significant improvement in learning after four years of college. No improvement in the areas of critical thinking, complex reasoning, and written communication. This equates to educational bankruptcy. If you're not going to put the time and effort into a higher level of thinking, then you might want to find a better way to spend $100,000 over the next four years. Serious leaders don't waste time and money, they have a game plan.

Colleges and universities that offer you country club amenities—hot tubs, fancy restaurants on campus, concierge services, flat screens in your dorm room, and wakeup calls—and have mediocre libraries and low-paid faculty, will not serve you well. Reach for intellectually challenging environments, wherever your career path leads you. The best leaders are lifelong learners; they focus on knowledge and always look to be challenged. Big leaders don't look for easy.

A Talent Marks survey found that 95 percent of college graduates do not have a clear understanding of their employment expectations or how to get a job. This survey went on to say that "college students who underestimate or dismiss the truly essential job expectations will come up empty in the job search and failure very likely waits." One North Carolina–based company who recently had 1,000 openings, some paying $105,000 a year, could not fill them.

> **Many university students are learning to think in distorted ways, and this increases their likelihood of becoming fragile, anxious, and easily hurt.**
> —*The Coddling of the American Mind* (2018) by Greg Lukianoff and Jonathan Haidt

Our world is now changing at mind-blowing velocity. Earth Incorporated can be brutal. To say we must learn to *embrace the chaos* becomes more relevant daily. Thomas Friedman, author of *The World is Flat* and *Thank You for Being Late*, calls this the "Age of Acceleration." Technology is causing cataclysmic changes in the workforce. Volatility, complexity, ambiguity, confusion and uncertainty now describe the economy you will walk into, and the throng of competition you will face for the desired high-paying jobs and flexible lifestyle you desire are no longer clearly defined. A college degree is not the guarantee it once was. Twenty-seven-year-old entrepreneur, founder of Imbellus Inc., and Harvard dropout Rebecca Kantar says, "For more than 50% of kids, college is net bad."

The corporate structure that your parents and grandparents may know so well has now begun to crumble in many sectors. Add to that the profound societal disruption caused by the COVID-19 pandemic and you should consider the following short list of attributes to focus on to meet new challenges:

➢ networking
➢ adaptability
➢ resiliency
➢ self-motivation
➢ bravery
➢ perseverance
➢ accountability
➢ personal branding
➢ collaboration
➢ empathy
➢ courage
➢ kindness
➢ decency

Let's take another brief look at select trends emerging in our ever-evolving demand economy:

➢ It's estimated that 20 percent of all skills are being reconfigured yearly; what you know today may need to be relearned every five years.

➢ A college freshman today may find their chosen degree redundant by graduation.

➢ Employees who are not focused on self-development, not engaged in immersive learning, and have no action plan for success will likely be unemployable in their lifetime.

➢ Resumes that are focused on personal achievements are receiving less attention; personality traits of kindness, humility, and servant leadership are often outweighing the usual long list of accomplishments.

➢ Current research indicates that work is changing faster than people are developing.

➢ Companies are reporting they can succeed or fail based on employee skills and personalities.

➢ The best leadership teacher in the world just may be *failure*. Effective leaders navigating a chaotic world often fail fast and fail often, but they *learn* from those failures.

➢ Tomorrow's leaders will delegate more as they focus on dilemmas, allowing people to make mistakes as part of their personal development.

Hardship is universal. Serious leaders don't look for easy. High-impact leaders ask big questions. Courageous and brave leadership is in high demand; average leadership is not. Effective leaders always step up, but mediocre leaders will wait. Game-changing leadership demands a serious, ongoing commitment.

Consider the following short list of emerging young leaders worth your review:

➢ Arthur Zang, Cameroon, rural health care

➤ Hasan Minhaj, United States, former Daily Show correspondent, Peabody Award winner

➤ Fatima al-Banawi, Saudi Arabia, Saudi storyteller

➤ Rasha Abu-Safieh and Bassma Ali, Gaza Strip, started GGateway

➤ Sabrina Cartabia, Argentina, lawyer and women's rights activist

➤ Sheku Kanneh-Mason, United Kingdom, young musician of the year, age nineteen

➤ Christine Figgener, Germany, marine conservation biologist, ending the age of plastic

➤ Sanna Marin, Finland's youngest Prime Minister, age thirty-five, COVID-19 fighter

➤ Ayana Johnson, marine biologist, climate optimist, and cofounder of the All We Can Save Project

➤ Apoorva Mehta, founder and CEO of Instacart, age thirty-four, who hired 300,000 workers in the gig economy in 2020 during the COVID-19 pandemic

A chaotic world can be an exciting and exhilarating one, an environment that can bring you significant happiness and success. Becoming an effective and catalytic leader will be the rewarding pathway. Remember that leadership is a commitment, a relentless commitment, and there are no genetics involved, so embrace the chaos, smile, and enjoy the journey!

Having problems is part of being alive. It is our difficulties and how we face them, more than our periods of contentment, that shape us throughout the course of our lives.
—Hector Garcia and Francesc Miralles, from their 2019 book titled *The Book of Ichigo Ichie, The Art of Making the Most of Every Moment*

You can live without Shakespeare and you can be happy without mastering Calculus, but you can't make it in this world without critical thinking skills and a lot of common sense.

Ultimately, your happiness and success will not depend on the things you have, but rather on how you choose to live your life. The quality of your life will rest on how you choose to live *emotionally.*

It's not the day you have to manage, but the moment. It's not the dragon you have to slay, but the fear. And it's not the path you have to know, but the destination. Thoughts become things, so be sure to pick the good ones.
—Mike Dooley, *Notes from the Universe*

At the end of your vocational career, you will find two questions to be rather profound. One, who did I become as a leader? Two, how many people did I help along the way?

Education should not be intended to make people comfortable; it is meant to make them think.
—Hannah Holborn Gray, President of the University of Chicago, 1978–1993

We stepped into the world as it was starting to fall apart.
—Simone Williams, Florida A&M University, commenting on the COVID-19 pandemic of 2020

Teach this triple truth to all: a generous heart, kind speech and a life of service and compassion are the things which renew humanity.
—Buddha, 500 BC

An education is the key to success. Bad habits and bad company will ruin you.
—Master Sgt. Roy Benavidez, Medal of Honor winner in Vietnam, Mexican American, part Yaqui Indian

I had to be cautious and follow my greater conviction.
—Laurent Duvernay-Tardif, MD and Kansas City Chiefs lineman, on why he missed the 2021 Super Bowl to treat COVID-19 patients

Hiyupo! (Follow me!)
—The first command always spoken by Lakota war leaders

Executives often trap themselves in
information bubbles, a result of their
overconfidence and outdated ideas about
leadership.
—Adam Bryant and Kevin Sharer, "Are You Really
Listening?" *The Harvard Business Review*, March/April
2021

Perhaps the greatest challenge business
leaders face today is how to stay competitive
amid constant turbulence and disruption.
—John Kotter, professor of leadership, Harvard
Business School

"Cheshire Puss," she began rather timidly,
"Would you tell me please which way I ought
to go from here?"

"That depends a good deal on where you
want to get to," said the Cat.

"I don't much care where," said Alice.

"Then it doesn't matter which way you go,"
said the Cat.
—Lewis Carroll, *Alice in Wonderland*

In the shopping malls, in the high school
halls, conform or be cast out. In the
basement bars, in the backs of cars, be cool
or be cast out.
—Rush, *Subdivisions*

Obviously, it's not black-and-white, but I do think women tend to be problem solvers and lead in a more participatory way. It's less hierarchal, and there's more listening and nurturing.
—Mary Robinson, the first female president of Ireland in 1990

Rapid recent advances in technology are forcing leaders in every business to rethink long-held beliefs about how to adapt to emerging technologies and new markets. What has become abundantly clear: in the digital age, conventional wisdom about business transformation no longer works, if it ever did.
—Abbosh, Nunes, and Downes, *Pivot to the Future: Discovering Value and Creating Growth in a Disrupted World*

A lack of workplace leadership contributes to 70% of employees not being engaged at work.
—Kevin Kruse, *Great Leaders Have No Rules*

There's only one way a business will win in the new world we're in. No other solution will work...growing and developing leadership talent of every single person throughout the organization faster than their competition.
—Robin Sharma, *The Leader Who Had No Title*

We're afraid of failure, of criticism, of making a mistake and getting caught. We worry that we'll lose our jobs if we stop managing and start leading.

—Seth Godin, *Tribes: We Need YOU to Lead Us*

Developing leaders who can navigate complexity is now a strategic priority and, if done well, a competitive advantage...we need to develop leaders with courage and compassion, consciousness and character... leaders set the agenda for the future.

—Anderson and Adams, *Mastering Leadership*

Leadership is like a muscle. The more intelligently you train, the stronger you get.

—John Ryan, President/CEO, *Center for Creative Leadership*

For us, warriors are not what you think of as warriors. The warrior is not someone who fights...the warrior is one who sacrifices himself for the good of others.

—Sitting Bull, Lakota Sioux Indian Chief, Indian leader at the Battle of Little Big Horn, 1876

Tell me, and I will forget.
Show me, and I may remember.
Involve me, and I will understand.

—Confucius, 450 BC

Leadership is about navigation–lots of choices, hazards and currents. Clarity of direction and flexibility of execution will be needed by leaders of the future.
—Bob Johansen, *New Leadership Literacies*

And life is all about warfare and a stranger's wanderings and the reward is oblivion. What then could possibly guide us? Only one thing: philosophy and this consists of keeping the divine spirit within each of us free from disrespect and harm, above pains and pleasure, doing nothing aimlessly or falsely.
—Marcus Aurelius, Roman Emperor, 161–180 CE

My Mom told me, "Fame is not important. Just stay humble, every day, any time, any day, just stay humble. Make sure you stay humble."
—Paul Chelimo, 2016 Olympian at 5,000 meters, Silver Medalist, Kenyan-born American

A leader is best when people barely know he exists; not so good when people obey and acclaim him; worst when they despise him.
—Lao-tzu, the *Tao Te Ching*

If you want to make everybody happy, don't be a leader, sell ice cream.
—Nick Saban, Football coach at the University of Alabama

The difference between *good leaders* and *great leaders* is not an issue of "more." They're fundamentally different people.
—Gautam Mukunda, Harvard Business School Professor

Stay away from negative people, they have a problem for every solution.
—Albert Einstein

The person who sweats more in training bleeds less in war.
— Ancient Spartans

If I know how you spend your time, then I know what might become of you.
—Johann Goethe, German statesman, poet, scientist, seventeenth and eighteenth centuries

When you stop living for luxuries, you understand the real meaning of life.
—Abdul Edhi, Pakistani humanitarian, 1928–2016, referred to as the world's "richest poor man"

Leaders need to understand what their people are thinking.
—Jeff Kortes, employee retention expert

There is no one more foolish than one who stops learning.
—Seneca, Roman philosopher and statesman, 65 AD

Great companies don't have skilled people and motivate them, they hire already motivated people and inspire them. People are either motivated or they are not. Unless you give motivated people something to believe in, something bigger than their job to work toward, they will motivate themselves to find a new job and you'll be stuck with whoever is left.

—Simon Sinek, executive leadership coach/author

ATTITUDE

Success is all about attitude.
—Tony Hsieh, CEO of Zappos and author of *Delivering Happiness*

The greatest human freedom is the freedom to choose one's attitude
—Viktor Frankl, Holocaust survivor

Attitude: posture; a mental position or feeling with regard to a fact or state

Great attitude is the key to great leadership.
This is the one thing you must have every day.
And it needs to be a *winning* attitude.
Outstanding leaders have a *winning attitude*; they are true champions of making good things happen.
You *must* develop a *winning attitude* and never compromise for anything less.
Attitude separates real leaders from everyone else.
Attitude attracts people to your ideas.
Attitude gets you through difficult times.
Attitude solves problems.
Attitude wins ball games.

Attitude makes money.
Attitude makes friends and creates networks.
Attitude instills self-confidence.
Attitude nurtures teamwork.
Attitude will either defeat or surrender to chaos.

All good leaders embrace a winning attitude or they go no-where fast, and excellence is not a skill, it's having and displaying a champion's attitude.

Without an all-out winning attitude, you will never achieve the outstanding results you're truly capable of. And in a chaotic world it's a matter of survive or thrive, your choice.

The business world is littered with very talented, bright, and ambitious people who never quite got it, never reached their goals, and couldn't understand why. While a positive outlook and winning attitude would seem to be the ultimate commonsense leadership attribute, careers get derailed very quickly when a personality of arrogance, conceit, and condescension surface. How many times have you heard the expression "drop the attitude"? Poor attitudes are a guaranteed dead end to effective leadership, irrespective of career path chosen.

The American poet and civil rights advocate Maya Angelou once said, "People will forget what you said, people will forget what you did, but people will never forget how you made them feel." While effective leadership has nothing to do with running a popularity contest, making a meaningful relational connection with people will absolutely be required. And a key component of that critical connection will be a winning attitude.

You will likely see students or business associates who are very controlling personalities—the ones who have to be the center of everyone's attention, all the time, in every situation. They have the boss mindset and may be viewed as strong leaders. It's one thing to be ambitious. It's totally another matter to have to control every situation you find yourself in. Do you really want to follow someone who is self-centered and lacks empathy and vision for others? Unfortunately, our business world is still burdened with leaders, people of influence, who get by with a lack of emotional intelligence, a lack of meaningful employee inclusion, and a dearth of deep listening. This isn't a winning attitude, and it's one you should totally avoid.

Always look inward. Make sure that you're on track with great attitude. Lead by example. You'll be surprised of the power of change a winning attitude can have on others. This is a key element to becoming a strong leader in a chaotic world—the power to motivate and inspire people, the ability to elevate others to extraordinary accomplishment. Attitude is the first place to start.

Your attitude has the power to change a lot of people and life events, creating meaningful change for both yourself and others. The greater business world needs your leadership, now.

And that leads us to the concept of embracing an attitude of servant leadership—helping others overcome obstacles, guiding work teams through the onslaught of complex dilemmas, becoming a multiplier, a genius maker, someone who has an intense focus on elevating coworkers to achieve uncommon results, leading with humility and kindness, and truly serving others.

The Real World

You may have graduated Phi Beta Kappa. Your graduate business degree may have come from a top business school. Last I checked, there were thousands with the same degree. Congrats on a superb accomplishment, but please understand, it's not all about you anymore. The greater business world is asking you to do one thing, and that is to move their enterprise forward, beginning your first day on the job. Your grades and resume to date are history. Your new employer is happy to have you, they just don't worship you, and bank on this—show up with arrogance, conceit, condescension, and weak interpersonal skills, and your corporate life span will be measured in nanoseconds. It starts with attitude.

The Japanese Way

It's very likely there is a made-in-Japan car in your driveway, perhaps a Toyota or a Honda. Their reputation for auto quality and engineering efficiency is almost legendary.

One of the hallmarks of Japanese business culture is the concept of "attitude" among its employees. In fact, that focus on attitude can be traced back to the Samurai warrior class in medieval Japan. In the Samurai period of the twelfth century, one's skill with a sword was often a matter of life and death, and it was acknowledged that the greatest masters of the sword were those who first learned and mastered the right attitude. It was said that a master swordsman could quickly judge the skill of an opponent by his attitude before that opponent made his first move.

When Japanese corporations interview job applicants, the first thing they look for and measure in that applicant is attitude. Candidates must have the right attitude, regardless of how otherwise brilliant or talented they may be. In promoting employees, Japanese companies rate attitude as the top attribute. In the Japanese business world, the right employee attitude includes such attributes as being a good listener, being polite, observant, humble, cooperative, and determined. This has given the Japanese business culture a decided advantage over numerous other countries. While most Western professional athletes learn very quickly that a great attitude is key to their successful performance, many Western business people have not yet learned just how powerful the right attitude can be in their personal and business lives. For those fortunate ones who have embraced the concept of winning attitude, they have found their lives to be healthier and far more productive. And fun!

> **You have creative intelligence, identify those areas that do not serve you well, eliminate negativity, avoid empty distractions.**
> —Deepak Chopra

Attitude over Obstacles

Talk about being in control of your life, just witness the accomplishment of Arizona State's Anthony Robles.

Anthony won an NCAA wrestling title in the 125-pound division with a final round 7–1 decision over defending champion Matt McDonough of Iowa. This capped an undefeated 36–0 season for Robles, who was also named the tournament's Outstanding Wrestler. And guess what?

Anthony Robles was born with only one leg.

Anthony wrestled with one leg, no prosthetic substitute.

What kind of an attitude do you think Anthony had to develop over the course of his young life to become not just the NCAA wrestling champion, but to be a shining example to others who face similar obstacles in life?

Remember, there are no halfhearted champions in life. Just ask Anthony Robles.

> **Your mind will take the shape of what you frequently hold in thought, for the human spirit is colored by such impressions.**
> —Marcus Aurelius, *Meditations*

Attitude Nurtures Teamwork

Without question, every successful leader in today's chaotic world has a laser focus on building great teams. These leaders will inspire and motivate their teams to stretch themselves to deliver extraordinary results, results that will exceed all expectations.

How do the most accomplished leaders drive team success? Is it my way or the highway? Are effective leaders mindful of the importance of meaningful and deep *listening*? What's their *attitude* in crafting excellence through teamwork?

Leadership expert Liz Wiseman has explored two distinct leadership styles. She categorizes them as either multipliers or diminishers, one with great attitude and empathy, the other with self-serving arrogance and manipulation.

Multipliers are the genius makers, focusing on everyone's strengths to accomplish desired results. Multipliers are great listeners, it's not all about them, their egos are in check, they work to make the team the best it can be. In contrast, Diminishers are self-centered, they see themselves as the hero in waiting, they're poor listeners, their egos are what's important, and it's more of a do-as-I-say operation than an all-inclusive team effort.

Who would you rather follow?

In 2017 US Navy SEAL Admiral William McRaven wrote a short but powerful book titled *Make Your Bed, Little Things That Can Change Your Life, And Maybe the World*. In that book Admiral McRaven related his 37 years in the SEALs to daily life lessons

WILLIAM R. MCKENZIE, JR.

for all. Consider the following quote on the power and need for strength and attitude in today's world:

> Life is full of difficult times. But someone out there always has it worse than you do. If you fill your days with pity, sorrowful for the way you have been treated, bemoaning your lot in life, blaming your circumstances on someone or something else, then life will be long and hard. If, on the other hand, you refuse to give up on your dreams, stand tall and strong against the odds—then life will be what you make of it—and you can make it great.

The message is very simple. A winning attitude and positive outlook will go a long way in getting you where you want to go. A winning attitude will tag you with strong leadership potential. A poor or mediocre attitude is a virtual program for failure, without question. Don't believe it? Cop a bad attitude for the next 30 days and see how much fun you have. Better yet, choose to have a winning attitude in everything you do and see what change it brings.

The greatest discovery of all time is that a person can change his future by merely changing his attitude.
—Oprah Winfrey

Embrace a winning attitude in all that you do. Embrace the chaos and enjoy the journey!

Making a Difference: Carl Vierling

By all accounts, Carl Vierling could be leading most any large company in America. The guy is a serious problem solver, always asking the big questions, the hard questions, demands a lot out of people, doesn't look for short cuts and, despite this commando persona, leads with kindness, decency and empathy. High-impact leadership is Carl's focus as he looks to create meaningful change in an area long ignored by many communities around the US: food insecurity.

Food insecurity is the nightmare almost 20 percent of US families face on a regular basis today, as they wonder if they will have enough food to eat on any given day. It affects all ages—children and the elderly perhaps most seriously. With the age group sixty-five-plus now outnumbering those five and under, its predicted that food insecurity among seniors will increase 50 percent by 2035.

So where does Carl fall into this leadership dilemma? He's busy forming relationships with decision makers, networking with community volunteers, and overcoming the inevitable skeptics. He's also working to, as he says, "blow up stereotypes" that are stuck in so many misinformed preconceptions about the poor and their associated hunger.

With a solid leadership background at one of the country's largest companies, holding a master's degree in human resources, a seminary degree, and pastoring an inner-city church along the way, Carl raised the issue of food insecurity in High Point, North Carolina in 2014, realizing that High Point was ranked #2 in the nation in food hardship at that time. Using his leadership skills in building problem-solving teams, focusing on sealing relationships with diverse citizen groups and giving a voice to people who had never had one, Carl was a "creative disruptive" force behind forming the Greater High Point Food Alliance in 2015.

By 2018 High Point's food insecurity ranking had fallen to number fourteen nationally and communities around North Carolina and beyond were asking for Carl's advice. Perhaps they heard how Carl's leadership had played a part in feeding 169,000 people with 2 million pounds of food dropped at a local church parking lot every Tuesday from 2015 to present. That $3.25 million in food value was just one of the many initiatives launched in High Point under Carl's guidance. Forming food education teams, urban farming initiatives, increasing food pantry access, initiating annual food summits for both students and the larger community, partnering with select hospitals and graduate schools for nutritional expertise—the list of High Point's proactive food/hunger initiatives under Carl's leadership grows longer.

Carl continues to lead by being present, focusing on his big three of advocacy, problem-solving, and relationship building. That's what serious leaders do and sometimes that makes people feel uncomfortable. Carl changes mindsets; he's a multiplier and a passionate servant leader. We need more creative disrupters like Carl Vierling in our increasingly chaotic and complex world.

Leadership lessons learned: passion, focus, serving others, compassion, teamwork, and creative disruption.

Attitude Key Points

> **Be a winner through your daily attitude**

> **Use mental muscle: be resilient and positive in the face of negativity**

> **Stay away from negative people, they can't help you**

> ➤ Focus on what's positive every day, not what brings you bad air

> ➤ Find something positive in your friends and make them feel special because of it

> ➤ Celebrate success, no matter how small; this breeds a winning attitude

Leadership Insights

> ➤ Emotional intelligence is how good leaders become great

> ➤ Be curious, ask big questions, listen

> ➤ Don't be a resistant leader, be open to change and personal growth

> ➤ Be honest with yourself, tell the truth

> ➤ Know what you're feeling and how to express that to others

People don't leave jobs. They leave toxic
work cultures.
  —Dr. Amina Aitsi-Selmi

Whatever you do, do enthusiastically and people will like you.

—Chris Martin, lead singer for *Coldplay*

PASSION

I put too much into this to pull out after one day.
—Lawson Craddock, US professional cyclist, after breaking his left scapula on day one of the 2018 Tour de France

Passion: strong feeling; emotions as distinguished from reason; an object of affection or enthusiasm.

Let Passion Drive You

Passion can present itself in a zillion different ways, and it often surfaces when we may least expect it. After all, the chaotic world we live in seems more conducive to an attraction-for-distraction agenda than a straight-line path to well-defined passionate goals.

Growing up in a family of seven—single mother and six children—now thirty-two-year-old Jonathan Seelig had no idea what his life's passion might be in that environment. As the youngest of three brothers and with no father figure to look up to, he struggled to find a happy place in school, preferring to act out. Jonathan's lack of focus and disruptive behavior led him to one juvenile home after another, beginning in the sixth grade. Jonathan was not a bad kid, just a confused and unsettled personality. He couldn't figure out why he had no father, food stamps were a must for his family, school wasn't his safe place, and he didn't like being told what to do by people he didn't know.

Eventually finding acceptance into a graphic design program at a local technical college, after stints in Job Corps and working as a forest fire fighter, the proverbial light came on. Jonathan had found his purpose in creating meaningful design, and through that new energy a desire to help others, just as so many anonymous people had helped him. Graphic design was a turning point; it became his passion.

With a newfound desire to reach and teach young students about a better life through food education with a nutritional focus, Johnathan set up a local nonprofit and created a unique program to make a difference, calling it Home Grown Heroes. His newfound passion began to ask the following questions:

1. How do we solve hunger and food insecurity in our community?

2. How do I passionately and effectively tell our story?

3. How do I harness community buy-in and participation?

4. How can I create an educational tool to impact young students?

5. How do I best communicate the absolute need to change our schools' food system?

There is no question about Jonathan's passion in pursuing his goal of creating a Read to Feed literacy program, a program designed to not only answer the questions above, but also to create a disruptive move to thinking aggressively and passionately about his communities' overall nutritional health.

Jonathan's wayward journey to find his passion to elevate his communities' understanding of better health through food education, using his talents in graphic design, illustrates what high-impact leadership can accomplish in a chaotic world. Jonathan's passion focuses on one of the biggest dilemmas society faces today: how to change our food IQ to achieve better health and happiness.

Passion in leadership is a big deal, a really big deal.

Passion is the link between who you are and how well you want to perform at some task, some subject, some sport or some identified business goal.

Don't have passion? Think you can lead effectively in a chaotic world with low energy? Then don't waste time trying to lead people. They won't follow you unless you are *passionate* about what you're doing and where you're going as a leader. Passionate leaders are strong communicators, great listeners, motivate and don't manipulate, ask the big and hard questions, and work to thrive in chaos, not merely survive.

How Can Passion Make a Difference?

Do you think eleven-year-old **Naomi Wadler** is passionate about responsible gun ownership? She spoke out against gun violence in front of eight hundred thousand people on March 24, 2018 at the March for Our Lives. She was representing African American women, victims of gun violence whose stories were not being told.

Do you think nine-year-old **Caesar Sant** is passionate about playing his violin? At age four Caesar could play Vivaldi and Tchaikovsky. At age five he had his first stroke. Partially paralyzed in 2014 after continued strokes from a rare genetic disorder, Caesar continues to find a way to practice two to three hours daily. He just will not give up playing the violin.

Do you think **Michael Phelps** was passionate about swimming? He once went five years without a day off from practice and won twenty-eight gold medals in Olympic competition. He is the most decorated Olympian in history.

Do you think **Dr. James Holland** was passionate about medicine? The founding father of chemotherapy in the 1950s ignored being called a research cowboy as he aggressively pursued finding a better treatment for pediatric leukemia. His team saw the death rate from acute lymphoblastic leukemia drop from more than 70 percent to 10 percent.

Do you think **Chieh Huang** is passionate about selling bulk groceries online? His six-year-old company, Boxed, has been called the "Sam's Club for millennials." Started in a garage, Boxed hit $40,000 in sales year one in 2014 and reached $100 million by 2018.

Do you think NBA Champion and MVP **Steph Curry** and his wife, Ayesha, are passionate about working to end childhood hunger, providing quality student education and providing safe places for children to stay active? The Curry's foundation, Eat. Learn. Play. is seriously focused on high-impact leadership and creating meaningful change for children in need.

Do you think **J. K. Rowling** is passionate about writing? Rejected twelve times, her *Harry Potter* books made her the first billionaire author. Yes, billionaire.

Do you think **Dan Cnossen** is passionate about the biathlon? A former Navy SEAL who lost both legs in combat in Afghanistan in 2009, he won the gold medal in the 7.5 kilometer sitting biathlon, one of five 2018 Paralympic medals he won in Pyeongchang, South Korea.

Do you think thirteen-year-old **Jordan Romero** was passionate about mountain climbing? He became the youngest climber to successfully summit Mt. Everest, the world's highest mountain at just under 30,000 feet. With one more climb in Antarctica, Jordan will become the youngest to achieve the revered "7 Summits." He set this goal when he was nine years old.

Do you think **Lynika Strozier** was passionate about biology? Growing up with serious learning disabilities, she went on to receive two master's degrees, specializing in plant DNA sequencing, and became a biology researcher at the Field Museum in Chicago before dying from COVID-19 in 2020 at the age of thirty-five.

Deval Patrick, abandoned by his father at age three, was raised by a single mom on the south side of Chicago, not exactly a country club setting. Earning a scholarship to a military academy in Massachusetts in the eighth grade, he would go on to Harvard College and Harvard Law School, graduating *cum laude* in 1982. Elected as the first African American Governor of Massachusetts in 2007 and serving until 2015, Deval Patrick's leadership was, and is, one of passion for racial equality, honesty, courage, humility, and curiosity. When asked to comment on the subject of leadership, Governor Patrick said:

> The qualities of a leader, regardless whether the setting is political or business or law, are basically the same: intellectual honesty, rigor, curiosity and humility. We need to stay curious and open to other people's ideas. I've been fortunate to surround myself with people who are smarter than me. They raise my game and have interesting ideas. It doesn't matter whether these people are

superiors or my subordinates. I just want to be around people who will challenge me to be better.

Like Governor Patrick, we know all strong leaders bring passion (rigor requires it!) to their business, whether that business is a high school, university, athletic team, new business startup, law firm, or Fortune 500 company. If those in charge, those in leadership positions, really intend to achieve desired results, they know they will have to bring passion to their operating agenda. They will have to be excited about the business strategy they have chosen and they will have to inspire and motivate their employees, their team mates, their faculty, and their students.

Leaders lead by example, they inspire, they motivate and if they don't have *passion* for what they're doing, you'll know it and you'll look elsewhere for strong leadership. So, if you don't have passion for what you do, don't expect anyone to follow you. You wouldn't.

Grit is passion and perseverance for long-term goals.
—Angela Duckworth, author of *Grit: The Power of Passion and Perseverance*

Look Around

In a world of ever-expanding chaos, leaders without absolute passion for what they do are destined to fail. Passion might be equated with high energy, relentless rigor, enthusiasm, strong emotion, excitement, or eagerness. One definition of a leader is someone who has followers. Who follows someone without passion, energy, excitement, and emotion?

Two of the most dynamic and passionate people in the area of leadership coaching and thinking today are Brené Brown and Jenn Lofgren. Dr. Brown delivers cutting-edge advice and insight into living a life of meaningful servant leadership, and her new book, *Daring to Lead*, is a must read. Ms. Lofgren founded Incito in Calgary, Canada, and specializes in executive leadership coaching. The below message from Dr. Brown and Ms. Lofgren conveys the power and expectation of authentic and passionate leadership via the concept of *vulnerability*:

> Daring leaders are highly strategic: they practice empathy and self-compassion, take risks, understand when to pull back or step forward. Look for opportunities to step into vulnerability. Effective leaders cannot work from a place of fear. Letting go of these fears require moving into a place of empathy and self-compassion. Only once you begin to work toward Creative Competencies will things open up to you as a leader. Stepping from Armored to Daring leadership and consequently from Reactive to Creative, requires a leader to operate from a place of vulnerability.

What does vulnerability mean and how does it relate to being a strong leader? Perhaps a passage from Amy Poehler's web series *Smart Girls: Ask Amy*, sums it up:

> It's very hard to have ideas. It's very hard to put yourself out there, it's very hard to be vulnerable, but those people who do that are the dreamers, the thinkers, and the creators. They are the magic people of the world.

Indeed, your leadership can be a magical trip, a passionate trip, a game-changing impact on the people you love and lead. Leadership bravery and courage require you to become vulnerable—open to, receptive to—all the challenge, the chaos, the discomfort, and the criticism that inevitably arises from the naysayers and victims. So, listen, learn, and move forward with passion and excitement into areas too few people are willing to go. This is what leadership is all about. Embrace the chaos and enjoy the journey!

> **The only way to be truly satisfied is to do what you believe is great work. And the only way to do great work is to love what you do. If you haven't found it yet, keep looking. Don't settle. As with all matters of the heart, you'll know when you find it.**
> —Steve Jobs

Don't confuse passion and excitement with a given type of personality. In other words, if you're reserved by nature, if you're not the outgoing type, if you're not a talker, that's fine. You can still be passionate about something that interests you. In fact, some of the most effective leaders are the ones who work behind the scenes, quietly making things happen without drawing a lot of attention to themselves, often giving recognition to fellow team members and staff.

The most effective leaders are often not the most vocal ones, but they are the ones with great attitude and great passion, however they choose to display those qualities.

Having passion for a cause does not automatically make you a leader. As you will see over the following chapters, leadership requires a number of well-defined traits, and passion is but one. You simply cannot be an effective leader without strong feelings for what you do. Passion is essential.

> **Do what you love to do. Anything is possible with hard work. You're always going to have hard moments but if you really want to do something, go for it.**
> —Geraint Thomas, 2018 Tour de France winner, thirty-two years old from Wales, only the third Briton to win the Tour de France.

Geraint Thomas not only found a way to embrace the chaos that truly is the Tour de France, he mastered that chaos with attitude and passion. He followed up his 2018 Tour de France victory with a second-place finish in 2019. He's enjoying the journey!

Remember, your leadership is defined by what and who you tolerate.

Making a Difference: Bethany Hamilton

Bethany was born February 8, 1990 in Kauai, Hawaii, to parents who loved to surf. Bethany easily took to the ocean water and watched her surfing abilities quickly progress. At age eight she won first place in a junior division of a Quicksilver surfing contest. At the same age, Bethany won first place in both a short board and a long board division at a tourney on the island of Oahu. At the age of nine, she began to compete more seriously, placing in the top three consistently at area surfing championships. She quickly picked up a major sponsor, Rip Curl, which helped her plans to become a professional surfer.

On October 31, 2003, Bethany went for an early morning surf with friends. Around 7:30 a.m., she was lying sideways on her surf board with her left arm dangling in the water. Suddenly, a fifteen-foot tiger shark attacked Bethany and ripped her left arm off just below the shoulder. Doctors said that if the shark bite had been a mere two more inches in, the attack would have been fatal. Losing almost 60 percent of her blood, Bethany was helped back to shore by friends, where a tourniquet was fashioned out of a surfboard leash and she was rushed to the local hospital. Her dad was scheduled for knee surgery that same day, but Bethany took his place in the operating room.

Just three weeks after losing her left arm, Bethany returned to surfing, teaching herself to surf with one arm.

The following year, in July 2004, Bethany won the ESPY Award for Best Comeback Athlete of the Year. She was also presented with a special courage award at the 2004 Teen Choice Awards. In the same year Bethany published her book, *Soul Surfer*, to detail her remarkable comeback from personal tragedy.

In 2005 Bethany took first place in the NSSA National Championships. In 2008, she began competing full-time on the Association of Surfing Professional World Qualifying Series, finishing third in her first competition against many of the world's best women surfers.

In 2010, *Soul Surfer* was released as a major motion picture.

Here are some of Bethany's key success strategies:
➢ Focus on what's important
➢ Face your fears
➢ Push yourself to do what you think you can't
➢ Be joyful

Bethany leads with passion. She did what all strong leaders do—they find a way to overcome significant obstacles to achieve the goals they have set. In the face of overwhelming odds against success, Bethany found a way to move forward with winning attitude and great passion for the sport of surfing.

Leadership lessons learned: passion, focus, overcoming obstacles, perseverance

Passion Key Points

> ➤ **Become enthusiastic about something important to you.**

> ➤ **Set goals and pursue them with energy and excitement.**

> ➤ **Study people you admire, and see how they achieve uncommon results.**

> ➤ **Believe in yourself.**

> ➤ **Challenge yourself.**

> ➤ **Find happiness in little things, and share that happiness with others.**

Leadership Insights

> ➤ **Big leadership is obsessed with where they're going.**

> Great leaders are strong on perspective and empathy, they feel for others.

> Serious leaders take responsibility for what they do wrong.

> Effective leaders are not afraid to fail, they know the importance of learning from failure.

> Leaders learn the importance of being the last to speak, the value of listening to others first.

If you chase two rabbits, both will escape.
—Unknown

FOCUS

The successful warrior is the average man with laser-like focus.
—Bruce Lee, one of the most influential martial artists of all time

Focus: to concentrate.

The ability to focus on the challenges at hand is critical to catalytic leadership.

A Running Focus Like No Other
If you know anything about the world of sports you know that African runners literally dominate the sport of running. It's not uncommon for these runners to take most of the top finishes in the distance races around the world, in times that virtually obliterate most of the elite field. A few examples:

> ➤ The 2019 Chicago Marathon male and female winners were both Kenyans, with Brigid Kosgei smashing the women's world record in two hours and fourteen minutes.

WILLIAM R. MCKENZIE, JR.

> The first sub-two-hour marathon was run in 2019 by Kenyan Eliud Kipchoge in Berlin.

> In 2020, a world record time of 26:11.00 in a 10K race was set by Joshua Cheptegei.

> A world record of 14:43 in the 5K distance was set by Beatrice Chepkoech in 2020.

> Joshua Cheptegei also set a men's world record in the 5K in 12:51 in 2020.

> In 2020 the men's world record in the half marathon was set by Kibiwott Kandie in 57:32.

> In 2021 Ruth Chengetich set the women's world half marathon record in 1:04:02.

Their success can certainly be traced to an incredible work ethic, where they run 150–175 miles a week at 6,000–8,000 feet elevation. It's not in their mentality to run easy. But equally important to their training schedule is the degree of *focus* they bring to each session. Here is what one of their coaches says. "The runners' lives are stripped of all diversion and comforts that Western athletes consider essential." In other words, their emphasis on training to be the best runners in the world has led them to bring an *intense focus* on simplifying their lives while training.

They have been known to live together in Spartan-like training camps, many without electricity or running water. They focus on running, and nothing else. There are no restaurants, no movie theaters, and no malls. They often leave their families for months at a time, live in primitive huts, go to bed at dark, and rise at first light. They eat simple foods. They train all day, every day. They run hard with no distractions. As one elite Kenyan runner said, "Running shoes, a rice cooker, and a mattress to sleep on. What else do you need?"

Western elite runners have attempted to train with the Kenyans over the years and many invariably cut their regimen short. Why? They simply cannot bring the same level of focus to their daily training. They can't keep up, mentally. The Kenyan runners seem to bring *more focus* to the sport than other competitive runners. Perhaps they listen to the following African proverb:

Every morning in Africa a gazelle wakes up.

It knows it must run faster than the fastest lion or it will be killed.

Every morning a lion wakes up.

It knows it must outrun the slowest gazelle or it will starve to death.

It doesn't matter whether you are a lion or a gazelle.

When the sun comes up, you better start running.

Simply put, they are *focused* like few other athletes in the world and their accomplishments are unparalleled. They know what focus is.

While you may feel the Kenyan story is an extreme example of focus to achieve results—and in many ways, it is—it by no means clouds the reality of what all good leaders need to have. If you want to be the best leader you can be, you will have to embrace the concept of *strong focus* as a key leadership attribute. In today's high velocity and chaotic economy, the ability to focus is not a luxury.

A Samurai Warrior

The amazing success story of Japan once again illustrates the power of intense focus relating to leadership and accomplishment. During the Samurai era (Japanese military aristocracy, twelfth and thirteenth century), one's diligent focus on matters of importance achieved virtual cult status. It amounted to "being Japanese," and became synonymous with completing any task undertaken. The Japanese believed themselves to be superior to anyone else in focus and work ethic. Those beliefs became culturally ingrained in Japanese society and would eventually emerge within Japanese business circles, giving their work force a competitive advantage over many Western business cultures. Their ability to bring intense focus to solving problems and listening to their customers has made them the perennial leaders in the automotive industry.

American Express

You may not know the name Kenneth Chenault, but the financial enterprise American Express certainly does. As only the third African American CEO of a Fortune 500 company, serving as both CEO and Chairman from 2001 to 2018, Chenault took a division of $100 million in sales and losing money to $700 million and profits. Dynamic leadership was key to his success. Chenault was a multiplier, focusing on creating winning teams and inspiring employees. "Leadership was my *focus*. I was happy that I was able to take people to achieve uncommon results."

Anything meaningful requires focus. The ability to focus will eventually set you apart from those who won't. Research tells us that when things get seriously tough, most people quit. Adversity then becomes your ally. Learn to focus, learn to filter and learn to drop the news-you-can't-use and other distractions.

Consider tech magnate Lei Jun, often referred to as having created the Apple of the East. With an undeniable *focus* on technology as a young boy in rural China in the 1980s, his father's monthly salary of $400 meant a $2,000 Apple II computer was a no-go. Not letting that get in the way, Lei Jun would wait for hours outside his school's meager computer lab, waiting for another student to miss his/her allotted turn. He once worked seventy-two hours straight without sleep just to use another's PC. "I even drew a keyboard on a sheet of paper and spent classes secretly practicing typing so I could use my time at the computer more efficiently," Lei says. Lei went on to finish his bachelor's in computer science in two years, joined a software company as an engineer, and became the CEO six years later. He went on to start his own tech company (Xiaomi) and reached $54 billion in value within eight years.

All strong leaders have the ability to focus on goals and objectives, despite sometimes challenging and chaotic circumstances.

It's a basic requirement for leadership success. You can't pass it off to someone else. You can't delegate focus. How good is your best teacher? How good is your best CEO? You have to know they're incredibly focused on what they do. That's a key reason they're so good at what they do. They bring concentrated effort to the subject every day. They're on top of their game. Their passion, attitude, and focus simply deliver what you consider to be outstanding results.

Ask them what drives them to be the best they can be. Ask them about leadership, about attitude, about passion, and about focus. *How do they navigate chaos?* Listen carefully to what they say. It's no accident they're as good as you think they are. Let them tell you why.

Focus Requires Filtering

In his acclaimed book on management, leadership and individual success—*The One Thing You Need to Know*—leadership consultant and author Marcus Buckingham writes:

> To thrive in this world will require of us a new skill. Not drive, not sheer intelligence, not creativity, but *focus*…to be able to focus well is to be able to filter well. Today you must excel at filtering the world. You must be able to cut through the clutter and zero in on the emotions or facts or events that really matter. You must learn to distinguish between what is merely important and what is imperative. You must learn to place less value on all that you can remember and more on those few things that you must never forget.

"We all struggle in the area of focus," writes former pro triathlete Brad Kearns. "Even motivated people see opportunities coming from so many different directions that it diverts their attention. When people are not focused, they make excuses beforehand to protect themselves from the pain of failure, and that becomes a vicious cycle."

The December 2013 cover of the *Harvard Business Review* highlighted the edition's featured article, "Focused Leaders." Author

Daniel Goleman writes that the primary task of leadership is defined as one of directing attention. To do that, Goleman says leaders must learn to focus their own attention. He argues that the popular belief that focusing requires the individual to filter out distractions while concentrating on just *one thing* is a leadership mistake. Neuroscience research shows that we focus in numerous ways and for different reasons. Goleman's solution reveals that leaders must recognize three areas of focus awareness—an inward focus, a focus on others, and an outward focus. He goes on to say that focusing inward and focusing on others aids leaders in building emotional intelligence, while focusing outward can improve the ability to create strategy, innovate, and manage organizations.

Executives who can focus effectively on others are known to emerge as natural leaders irrespective of business or social rank. They make the important emotional connection with subordinates and team members while not running a popularity contest. And this can be a serious challenge. Research indicates that as people move up through the business ranks, their ability to maintain critical personal connections begins to suffer. As their sphere of focus narrows, they become the leaders more likely to interrupt or dominate the conversation, the ones who lose social sensitivity, and are apt to place the blame for personal shortcomings somewhere else.

Leaders with a solid outward focus are both good listeners and good questioners. They ask the big questions; they ask the hard questions. They are true visionaries who can imagine how the action they take today will play out in times to come.

Information overload is perhaps the biggest challenge to leadership focus today. As far back as 1971 the Nobel Prize winning economist Herbert Simon wrote, "Information consumes the attention of its recipients, hence a wealth of information creates a poverty of attention." Fast forward to today, and author Goleman writes,

> Practically every form of focus can be strengthened. What it takes is not talent so much as diligence—a willingness to exercise the attention circuits of the brain just as we exercise our analytic skills and other systems of the body...Yet attention is the basis of the most essential of leadership skills—emotional, organizational, and strategic intelligence...The constant onslaught of incoming data leads to sloppy shortcuts—triaging our email by reading only the subject lines, skipping many of our voice mails, skimming memos and reports. Not only do our habits of attention make us less effective, but the sheer volume of all those messages leaves us too little time to reflect on what they really mean.

On September 16, 2018, Kenyan runner Eliud Kipchoge set a new marathon world record in Berlin in an amazing time of 2:01:39. When a reporter asked him how, at a time when he is suffering the most, when he is physically drained, he simply smiles, Kipchoge replied, "It is at these moments that I *focus* on the goal. My emotions abound. I know I can control them and then my whole body will smile."

This Is What Leaders Do
Keep focus in mind. Focus and filter through the clutter of everyday life, eliminate wasteful time, and you can experience exciting success as you develop strong leadership skills. Remember,

effective leadership is a commitment. There are no born leaders. There is no genetic link.

Embrace the chaos, learn to work in areas of discomfort, do what others will not do. Understand that your world is likely full of information overload and it's easy to be "driven to distraction." Effective leaders know how to filter out the useless and focus on what's important.

Remember the Kenyan runners, look at your best teachers, watch your most successful coaches, and listen to your accomplished business mentors. They all exhibit great focus in what they do. They choose to thrive, not merely survive.

Learn to focus on important goals and objectives. It doesn't mean you have to live in a box. Being focused is about staying on a deliberate path, owning that path, making it your path. It'll pay big dividends for you. So, embrace today's chaos and enjoy the journey!

> **If a man does not know to what port he is steering, no wind is favorable.**
> —Seneca, ancient Roman philosopher, statesman and dramatist, 4 BC–65 AD

Making a Difference: Marin Morrison

Marin was raised in Florida, and at an early age took to the swimming pool quickly, like a lot of children in the Sunshine State. By the time she was in the fifth grade, her family moved to Atlanta where she joined the Swim Atlanta team. At age thirteen she beat seventeen-year-old Amanda Weir, who would go on to win two silver medals in the 2000 Olympics. Her coach said, "Marin has all the tools, speed, desire, coachability. We're pretty much talking unlimited potential."

While attending Collins Hill High School in Suwanee, Georgia, Marin set numerous school records and appeared to be well on her way to the 2008 Olympic Trials. However, at the state high school championships, Marin became ill and finished way off her expected times. She complained of a searing headache and vomited on the pool deck. A visit to a neurologist resulted in the discovery of a plum-sized brain tumor. The tumor was successfully removed and declared benign. But months later, the blurred vision and pain returned, and an aggressively growing tumor was discovered once again. There was no choice but to operate. The prognosis was bleak, and Marin was left paralyzed on her right side. The tumor was malignant.

Even with this horrifying news, Marin remained determined and focused. Her first words following intense speech therapy were, "Can I still swim?" In the fall of 2005, after grueling radiation and further rehab, the doctors called Marin's parents and told them nothing else could be done, Marin would not survive, and they should enjoy their last days with their daughter. Marin turned to her parents and said, "Don't believe them. I'll keep fighting."

For more than a year the tumor began to shrink. Marin returned to the pool, even with her right side paralyzed. She developed drills that allowed her to use her left side. She rejoined the high school swim team. Then, swimming for a disabled swim team, Marin set two national records, qualifying her for the 2008 Paralympic Games in Beijing. But doctors hadn't given her long to live. Just prior to the Beijing games, in May 2008, Marin had to undergo a fourth surgery. She became confined to a wheel chair, too sick to fly to Beijing. With help from friends and the US Olympic Committee, Marin and her family made it to Beijing. Too sick to stay in the athlete's village, Marin stayed with family in the Beijing Hilton.

On race day, Marin's dad rolled her wheel chair to the starting lane and helped her enter the water, readying her for the 100-meter backstroke. The gun went off and Marin struggled in lane seven. Partially blind, partially paralyzed, but with an indomitable will to succeed, Marin finished her race with the crowd roaring in amazed excitement. Her dad was waiting at the finish, and behind a red, white, and blue eye patch, Marin exclaimed, "I did it."

Marin Morrison, age eighteen, died on January 2, 2009, three months after achieving her Olympic dream. Do you think that Marin was focused?

Leadership lessons learned: passion, focus, winning attitude, overcoming obstacles

Focus Key Points

➢ **Concentrate on what's important and filter out what's not.**

➢ **Realize that achieving and leading requires discipline.**

➢ **Be aware of distractions and learn to move through them.**

➢ **Remember the African proverb about the lion and the gazelle.**

➢ **Master the technology paradox.**

➢ **Learn from Marin Morrison.**

WILLIAM R. MCKENZIE, JR.

Leadership Insights

➢ **Creating the right environment is critical to big, effective leadership.**

➢ **Empathy and perspective are two essential leadership must-haves.**

➢ **Most companies will *not* teach you how to lead.**

➢ **Serious leaders are not afraid to make mistakes and should nurture that same feeling in those they lead.**

➢ **Leaders look to help people be at their natural best.**

Defer no time, delays have dangerous ends.
—Shakespeare, *Henry VI*

URGENCY

Everyone admires the bold; no one honors the timid.
—Robert Green and Joost Elffers, *48 Laws of Power*

Urgency: importance, requiring swift action

Acting with a Sense of Urgency
In their fascinating book *48 laws of Power*, authors Green and Elffers made a relatively simple but powerful observation when they said, "Everyone admires the bold; no one admires the timid." Bold leaders have an attendant sense of urgency about what they want to do. Otherwise, nothing gets done in a timely fashion, schedules fall apart, the people you want to lead don't see you getting things done, and your effectiveness as a leader is greatly diminished.

Effective leadership is not about living your life on an all-out roller coaster ride daily, trying to knock off one project after another at the speed of light. How much can I get done? How fast can I do it? That's not the point. Good leaders are certainly in tune to being bold and getting things done quickly, but they do so with organization and planning. They do so with attitude, passion, focus, and urgency. It's the concept of doing "right things right" as opposed to doing "right things wrong." You want to work efficiently and smart, not hard. Again, it's a matter of surviving or thriving in chaos.

Certainly, there are times and projects that call for a longer and more protracted time line, and leadership is not about spinning your wheels at warp speed every day. Good leaders do a great job of planning, setting strategy, and putting the right team together. They know where they're going and how they're going to get there, even through failure (in fact, the best leadership teacher just may be failure). Things keep moving forward, the goal is in mind—attitude, passion, and focus are at work, and so is a sense of urgency.

There are other descriptive adjectives that can be substituted for urgency—gravity, necessity, tenacity, persistence, and determination—but the common denominator is moving swiftly with purpose. A more in-depth look at this key leadership attribute reveals a number of strategic learnings that every effective leader will need to lift their team to desired outcomes.

Embracing a sense of urgency can be seen to consist of two key elements. One, recognizing the extent that we perceive that a problem or situation is important. Two, whether the response dictates a more deliberate approach versus more urgent action. Teams that are lacking a needed sense of urgency will require new habits of thinking, perceiving, and acting.

While working in the complex and chaotic world we have come to know, leaders will want to focus on team action that is in proportion to the required urgency. How important is the problem at hand? What's really at stake? What are the desired outcomes and how difficult will the path to resolution be? The most common problem here is one of potential team whiplash and lack of focus, where the leader(s) show too much emotion too often or too little, leaving the team wondering what's really at stake.

Clarifying the consequences of failing to problem solve with a sense of urgency is a leader's responsibility. A team's potential poor performance can be rooted in an avalanche of excuses, and consequences have to be real. Status quo will likely set in when a team loses its intensity and they eventually find themselves out in the cold.

Courageous leaders will use a sense of urgency to persevere despite the problem-solving pain often encountered. Experience shows that acting with urgency can help push teams through that pain rather than succumb to it. Leaders have to work with a combination of intellect and clarity for focused action by their team.

One very important piece of effective leadership to remember when working through complex team goals, with a sense of urgency, is the value of recognizing team members who exhibit this attribute. Recognizing and celebrating even incremental successes will go a very long way in building high-performance teams and employees in a culture of exemplary leadership.

The Little Big Horn: Urgency and Survival

Sitting Bull and Crazy Horse, the two best known leaders of the Lakota Sioux Indian nation, wasted little time in setting battle strategy against General George Armstrong Custer and the 7th US Cavalry in June of 1876. Having lived through one broken US Government treaty after another, having seen their tribal lands invaded and ravaged repeatedly, having seen their magnificent bison herds slaughtered by the tens of thousands, and having witnessed what today we call genocide, Sitting Bull and Crazy Horse had an *extreme sense of urgency* to plan perhaps what would be their last stand against the relentless invasion of white settlers.

It wasn't enough that they were smarter in battle tactics than Custer and his officers; it wasn't enough that the Sioux were more focused on survival than their white counterparts, the ultimate winner of the Battle of the Little Big Horn would need to bring more battle strategy into sharper focus *faster* than Custer and company. On that hot day in June 1876, the leadership edge went to Sitting Bull and Crazy Horse in virtually every aspect of warfare known at that time.

Sitting Bull was extremely organized in both short- and long-term strategy. Historians have characterized him as intelligent, wise, and charismatic. He was able to bring several disparate Indian tribes into cohesive teamwork through his reputation as a warrior (leader), as a strong communicator, and as a leader with vision. He didn't waste a lot of time. Once he established a strategy, once he crafted a plan, the execution of that plan happened quickly and completely.

Crazy Horse always displayed imaginative initiative in battle, and there was no mistaking his sense of urgency when it came to the survival of his people. Admired for his humility and concern for his people, he was revered for always focusing on the needs of the very young and the elderly of his tribe. As Lakota historian Joseph Marshall III writes, "He had a lifelong habit of taking care of elderly people first. Whenever he hunted, before he took meat to his own family, he made sure the elderly had enough to eat."

Water Man, one of the few Arapaho warriors who fought that day with Crazy Horse, said, "He was the bravest man I ever saw. He rode closest to the soldiers, yelling to his warriors. All the soldiers were shooting at him, but he was never hit." The Sioux warrior Little Soldier said, "The greatest soldier in the whole battle was Crazy Horse." Crazy Horse was remembered as someone always willing to take the lead.

Sitting Bull and Crazy Horse, along with numerous other very capable Indian leaders, completely annihilated General Custer's famed 7th Cavalry at the Big Horn River in 1876. While it was a short-lived victory for the besieged American Indian, it serves as a crystal-clear example of outstanding leadership, embracing the qualities of teamwork, focus, and urgency to accomplish a defined goal; in this case, the ultimate goal is one of personal and family survival. Custer was simply out led by his Indian counterparts. Their sense of urgency to survive must have been far greater and in sharper focus than Custer imagined and planned for. Sitting Bull and Crazy Horse were bold leaders, there was no room for the timid in their culture, and history regards them both as exhibiting some of the very strongest of leadership qualities.

Their leadership that day, their sense of urgency, their ability to master the inevitable chaos of war was in direct proportion to the situation they faced.

> **Success most often goes to the person who sees that he has made a mistake and quickly changes. Winning leaders are invariably good "game coaches," because they are the first to see how things are going, then quickly figure out why, and then they make the appropriate changes.**
> —*Machiavelli on Modern Leadership*, Michael Ledeen (noted Wall Street Journal writer)

Note the phrase above, "then quickly figure out why." It's the urgency factor surfacing again. Sitting Bull and Crazy Horse were superb "game coaches" at Little Big Horn. They had to be. It was a matter of survival.

Dell Computer: Change or Perish

Once known as the direct sales innovator in home computers, Dell developed a business culture often referred to as a culture of bureaucracy, meaning that over time Dell essentially lost their ability to change quickly to successfully address market demands. Their business model was simply too unresponsive, too slow, and too nearsighted in an expanding chaotic technology market. Profits fell a staggering 51 percent in one quarter and the trend continued. Michael Dell, the once highly regarded founder, was at one time named one of worst leaders by *Business Week* magazine, who cited him for "Worst Reaction Time" for his inability to move away from and transform the lethargic Dell culture into a more responsive organization. While Dell was mired in slow motion, rival Hewlett-Packard increased sales 26 percent. Dell's sales then fell another 14 percent.

Michael Dell finally got the message and was quoted as saying he would change the company into one that was "bold in thinking and *swift in action.*"

➤ *Swift in action*
➤ *Quickly figuring out why*
➤ *Good game coaches*
➤ *Making the appropriate changes*

The ability to act decisively and with urgency is a leadership skill you will need to develop as you navigate complexity and chaos. Concentrate on becoming dynamically resilient. Leaders encounter challenges and demands daily. The stress leaders often face can be physical, mental or emotional. The best leaders find themselves with the ability to make adjustments and reset quickly.

Urgency can certainly be linked to initiative. People showing initiative in any endeavor seem to display an inherent sense of taking charge to get something done. They don't wait to be asked, they don't waste time, they don't procrastinate, they don't forget—they move on it *now*.

The best leaders today embrace the chaos. They work to exploit problems and create meaningful opportunities while others only see problems as problems.

Moving Your Team with Urgency

Don't be surprised if you encounter a team without a healthy sense of urgency. It will happen eventually, and these teams will require new habits of thinking, perceiving, and acting. As their leader you will want to consider the following.

What's at stake? Is the problem, or dilemma, acute or benign? What's your message to the team? Is your response in proportion to the importance of the challenge? Remember, leaders communicate by example so your emotional response is key. Are you causing emotional whiplash by showing too much emotion too often? If your emotional response is too fragile, then the team begins to wonder what's really at stake, so be careful to deliver your message to the team with the level of importance it deserves.

Always clarify the consequences to your team and be careful not to let the status quo settle in. Use urgency to push through the tough stuff, move through the pain of problem-solving, and always recognize team members who exhibit a sense of urgency and work to help others. Even if the success is just incremental, highlight accomplishment and celebrate results.

Effective leaders will embrace the chaos caused by their team's temporary loss of morale and focus by finding a path to successful completion. It's what they do best in areas of extreme discomfort and uneasiness.

Your time is limited, so don't waste it living someone else's life. Don't be trapped by dogma, which is living with the results of other people's thinking. Don't let the noise of others' opinions drown out your own inner voice. And most important, have the courage to follow your heart and intuition.

—Steve Jobs

Making a Difference: Jermaine Wilson

It's often said that perhaps the best leadership training comes through *failure*. Given that leaders eventually find themselves in areas of unexpected uncertainty, confusion, complexity, and accelerating change, the opportunity to make serious misjudgments is not uncommon. The key to navigating the chaos and emerging as a stronger person and leader involves both perseverance and a serious desire to learn from that failure.

Jermaine Wilson knows failure all too well. Growing up in government housing in a crime-infested neighborhood in Leavenworth, Kansas, Jermaine was expelled from school at age eleven, ran away from home, began dealing drugs and found himself in prison at age fifteen. Trying to escape upped his prison sentence from two years to four. Free at age nineteen, he once again began using and selling drugs. Arrested again, he was back in prison, alone with a Bible and surrounded by murderers and rapists. He quickly sobered up, realizing he had leadership qualities to offer if he would only focus them in a positive direction.

Jermaine changed his total mindset, and he decided to improve himself and use what he decided were his God-given leadership abilities.

With his criminal records expunged in 2015, he started a nonprofit to mentor youth and serve the homeless, began speaking to youth groups and working to strengthen the bonds between law enforcement and his community.

A friend recommended that he run for Mayor of Leavenworth and with the encouragement of his wife, Jermaine ran and became Mayor in 2019 at the age of 31.

With a focus on servant leadership and a compassionate mindset, Jermaine is a leadership example of overcoming obstacles, persevering and learning from failure to create high-impact change for his community.

Leadership lessons learned: learning from failure, passion, perseverance, attitude, and focus

Urgency Key Points

➢ **Be bold and aggressive in a good way.**

➢ **Don't delay decision making.**

➢ **Up your energy level when completing a goal.**

➢ **Initiative is important, take charge and move a project forward.**

➢ **See if a to-do list works for you, or maybe a not-to-do list.**

➢ **Move through distractions, don't get side-tracked and delayed.**

Leadership Insights

> ➤ In today's chaotic world leadership *competency* is only half the game; leadership *character* is the other half.

> ➤ Great leadership demands wisdom, self-knowledge, courage, conviction, humility, and character development.

> ➤ The top two challenges facing business leaders today are escalating complexity and building the creative capacity in leadership to deal with it.

> ➤ Leadership skills for the future will be immersive learning, clarity, dilemma flipping, empathy, and becoming comfortable in an arena of discomfort.

> ➤ Leaders will need to see themselves as multipliers, genius makers, capable of elevating their teams to uncommon results.

WILLIAM R. MCKENZIE, JR.

Teamwork. They slam that word at you
every other minute. *Teamwork. Teamwork.
Teamwork.*
   —Marcus Luttrell, decorated US Navy SEAL, author
   of **Lone Survivor**

TEAMWORK

Leadership isn't just about the talent at the top. It's about you and your team working together to achieve cohesive outcomes.
—Center for Creative Leadership

Teamwork: the activity of a number of persons acting in close association as members of a unit.

Ask any astute business person today what key attributes an employer looks for in future employee hiring and you will invariably hear the word *teamwork* mentioned.

Employers must hire people who can work together as a team.

It's not a nice-to-have quality in the work force. It's an essential necessity that, if absent, will eventually spell failure for any given business today.

Why is teamwork so important to the principles of excellent leadership? Why do all *effective* leaders focus on outstanding teamwork as part of their personal operating behavior? Listen to what American researcher and executive advisor Liz Wiseman writes in her bestselling book *Multipliers, How the Best Leaders Make Everyone Smarter:*

> Multipliers…leaders who use their intelligence to
> amplify the smarts and capabilities of the people
> around them. Diminishers…the idea killers, the
> energy sappers, always need to be the smartest
> one in the room.

It's a New Day

The days of the General commanding the troops in business, industry, school, and the like are long over. Getting desired results
in any business enterprise no longer relies on a single hero and a
thousand helpers. Why? Life is simply too complex and too difficult for any one person to totally run the show. It can't be done
effectively or successfully by any one individual. In a fast-paced
world, in a chaotic world, working in a team concept can be enor-
mously helpful. It's a defined necessity for any leader to develop
and nurture solid teamwork. Effective leaders can't do without it.

Harvard Business School professor Amy Edmondson has
coined the phrase *psychological safety.* In her words:

> Simply put, psychological safety makes it possible
> to give tough feedback and have difficult conversa-
> tions without the need to tiptoe around the truth.
> In psychological safe environments, people believe
> that if they make a mistake, others will not penalize
> or think less of them for it. They also believe that
> others will not resent or humiliate them when they
> ask for help or information. Psychological safety
> does not imply a cozy situation in which people
> are necessarily close friends. Nor does it suggest
> an absence of pressure and problems.

Simply put, teamwork is critical to any measure of personal and collective success, and high-impact leaders must know how to develop it and use it constructively to achieve targeted results.

It's less *me* and more *we*.

I didn't think I could get 4 stages here. I really want to congratulate the whole team because it's their victory as well. Everyone has worked really hard and the work is paying off.
—French professional cyclist Arnaud Demare on winning his fourth stage at the 2020 Giro d'Italia.

Climbing the World's Tenth-Highest Mountain

If ever there was a sport that required incredible teamwork to achieve success its high-altitude mountain climbing, or mountaineering. Imagine what it took Arlene Blum in 1978 to lead the first ever women's attempt to climb the world's tenth-highest mountain, the Himalayan giant Annapurna, at 26,545 feet. She had to begin by picking a top-rate climbing team, women that not only had all the technical skills required, but women who could put personal ego aside and realize that individually, they may or may not make the mountain's summit. That call would eventually rest with Arlene as the climbing leader. But there would have to be an incredible amount of teamwork to have any chance at success against such a dangerous and challenging mission. Her team was successful, but only a few of the climbing team made it successfully to the summit. The climb took the ultimate in sacrifice and teamwork, but the goal was achieved.

The Ultimate Team: US Navy SEALs

You've heard of the Navy SEALs (Sea-Air-Land)? One of the most effective fighting teams in military history, here is what one nationally known consultant says:

> The SEALS are without doubt one of the highest-performing organizations (teams) on the planet. The secret ingredient is that every SEAL is a leader/teacher, engaged in continuous, interactive teaching and learning.

The SEALS operate in teams. They train together in teams for a minimum of eighteen months, and then continue their teamwork as mission orders demand.

They don't conduct solo missions. They always function as a well-trained team, and that is perhaps their greatest strength.

Their military accomplishments are legendary for the degree of danger and operating difficulty they encounter and successfully overcome. They are the military team that vows to leave no team member behind, whether dead or alive. That's the ultimate commitment to teamwork.

On April 9, 2009, a three-man SEAL team rescued American boat captain Richard Phillips from Somali pirates by firing three simultaneous nighttime gunshots from a moving boat in choppy water. Three shots, three kills. This type of skill level is truly amazing, the necessary teamwork to accomplish such a feat even more so. Working together, following a carefully crafted plan, and believing in each team member's ability and focus, these SEALs made the seemingly impossible a reality. Their secret is a *focus* on mental conditioning and *teamwork*.

In the early morning hours of May 1, 2011, SEAL teams dropped into a walled compound in Abbottabad, Pakistan, a stealth mission to take out the world's number-one terrorist, Osama bin Laden. Minutes later it was mission accomplished. Bin Laden was dead and all SEAL teams were back to home base unharmed.

Once again, we see the power of teamwork in the most difficult and dangerous of circumstances.

Want to lead like a SEAL? Take a look at the six key values SEALs focus on:

➢ Put teammates first: *How do I treat others? How do I fit into the team? What is my responsibility?* No matter your profession or goal, ask yourself these questions.

➢ Second-guess yourself: Quitting something happens to everyone. Ask who you are.

➢ Allow yourself to fear: Fear is a shared experience, and you'll get a lot of energy from those around you. It's ok to be afraid. Recognizing that is the first step to overcoming it.

➢ Control your emotions physically: Ask a friend to study your posture when you're happy or content. Then practice it, over and over. Your psyche will follow your body.

➢ Break big goals into small targets: Try to stay in the present. How do you eat an elephant? One bite at a time.

➤ Have faith in yourself: *This is the most critical part of mental toughness. Have faith that you'll figure it out.*

Now consider what two Navy SEALs, Jocko Willink and Leif Babin, write about leadership and teamwork in their book, *Extreme Ownership, How U.S. Navy SEALs Lead and Win:*

➤ A leader must be humble but not passive; quiet but not silent.

➤ A leader must be close with subordinates but not too close.

➤ Leaders must never get so close that the team forgets who is in charge.

➤ A leader does not gloat or revel in his or her position.

➤ A leader must be confident but never cocky.

➤ A leader must be calm but not robotic.

Navy SEAL Admiral William McRaven has said this about teamwork:

I learned early on in SEAL training the value of teamwork, the need to rely on someone else to help you through difficult tasks. No SEAL could make it through combat alone and by extension you need people in your life to help you through difficult times.

Google recently conducted a five-year study on high performing teams, called Project Aristotle, and found that out of five dynamics that set very successful teams apart, the number-one factor was psychological safety, meaning it was ok for team members to feel safe in taking risks and being vulnerable in front of each other. Having difficult conversations and giving tough feedback without negative repercussion elevated team accomplishment.

Maximum Leadership and Team Effectiveness

High-impact leadership author Alison Levine writes in her extraordinary book, *On The Edge:*

> In today's volatile and competitive business environment, leaders are required to make critical decisions when the conditions surrounding them are far from perfect. The survival of your team will depend on it.

> The way you deal with the weak link on your team could mean the difference between success and failure. Weak associates are not hard to identify. Weak associates are also a liability. Don't spend a lot of time trying to nurture and elevate weak behavior. It will drag your team down. There's very little to gain in moving someone from weakness to average. A leader's challenge is to craft the very best team possible from the beginning. Rarely will you have the luxury of infinite time to assemble your team. Complacency will kill you.

Great leaders find unexpected ways to bring out the best in themselves and others. Do whatever you have to do in order to make everyone on your team feel like they are valuable contributors. And instead of expecting others to overcome a weakness, get creative and find ways to help them compensate, which often involves leveraging hidden talents. Ultimately, you and your team will be stronger for it.

Levine goes on to say:

Timing, proximity, and a common goal are not enough to form a cohesive team. Teamwork is about looking out for one another, helping one another, and winning together. And if you're lucky enough to be in a position where you have some say in choosing your team, look for the Three Es: experience, expertise and ego.

Acknowledging the complexity of the business world today, it's not uncommon to find cultures dominated by intense pressure to achieve and meet short-term goals. Within that high-anxiety environment many leaders value the absolute high performer and ignore other team members. The focus becomes centered on identifying the biggest winners, and lesser accomplishments may result in terminations. This atmosphere ultimately becomes corrosive and cut-throat. As Simon Sinek outlines in his new book, *The Infinite Game*:

The problem is, the toxic team members are often more interested in their own performance and career trajectories than they are with helping the whole team rise. And though they may crush it in the near term, the manner in which they achieve their results will often contribute to a toxic environment in which others will struggle to thrive. Indeed, in performance-obsessed cultures, these tendencies are often exacerbated by leaders who encourage internal competition as a way to further drive performance.

Never underestimate the value of extraordinary teamwork in becoming a great leader. Leaders take serious ownership when teams sometimes fall apart. Rebellious or wayward teams require leaders who can and will admit to problems, own the challenges and seek the necessary help to fix them. They acknowledge the problem, look for the source, take ownership, ask for help, elicit input from team members and lead from within, looking to the team for bigger solutions.

Great leaders embrace the chaos and know the journey has great rewards!

Success requires leadership. Leadership requires teamwork. It's a pretty simple equation.

Making a Difference: Vanessa Parmenter

When students enter Vanessa Parmenter's high school English Literature class at Greensboro, North Carolina's Newcomers School, they walk into an atmosphere of high energy, high intellect and unquestioned passion for teaching and learning. These students will need all the attention Vanessa can give them, not because they are learning deficient, but because each one of them is either an *immigrant* or *refugee*. English is their second language and while some are more proficient than others, each one will require all of Vanessa's intellect and passion for teaching.

Twenty-six students in a class, six different languages. It's a leadership moment for Vanessa every day.

How does Vanessa tackle this challenge? She does what every effective leader does. She shows up with grit, that critical combination of *passion* and *perseverance*. And Vanessa knows grit.

When she was a young girl living in her native Australia, she was diagnosed with a serious spinal condition that, if left untreated, would have been fatal. At age twelve Vanessa endured a delicate eight-hour surgical procedure and six months in a full body cast. While the surgery was successful and the rehab was long and tiring, perhaps the biggest challenge was absorbing the finger pointing and teasing from other children. Vanessa just returned the curious looks with a smile and a laugh, traits she now delivers to her multinational classroom.

Vanessa would go on to pursue her love of literature and history, graduating from the University of Sydney with a bachelor's degree in education and a focus on the humanities. She was student teaching at the university at the age of nineteen when most students were content with a normal course load.

Vanessa's next challenge was to weather a lengthy immigration process to gain US citizenship and accept the teaching position she had been offered. With that mission completed Vanessa quickly excelled in the classroom, as did her students. Twice named "Teacher of the Year," writing curriculum for high school English teachers and working to start the Newcomers School, Vanessa has done what all effective leaders do—create meaningful change.

Vanessa is a high-impact leader, even though she doesn't see herself as such. She teaches her multinational students what's possible, instills confidence, a love of learning, and how education can make a difference in their lives.

After all, that's what serious leaders do, they make a difference.

Leadership lessons learned: perseverance, focus, passion, compassion, productive disruption

Teamwork Key Points

> **Learn to work with and through people; not over, under and around them.**

> **Remember, it should be less me, more we.**

> **Be like a Navy SEAL: put teammates first.**

> **Many problems are simply too big for one person.**

> **Use your athletic experience: mediocre team or great team?**

> **Become a multiplier, work to elevate your team(s) to higher performance.**

Leadership Insights

> **The most effective leaders use second person pronouns (like *you* and *your*) instead of first-person pronouns (like *I*, *me*, and *my*).**

➢ **Leaders must focus on integrity, focusing on what's right and not what's easy, while building trusting relationships.**

➢ **A leadership mindset of motivating others requires you to be present, to be mindful, and to be authentic.**

➢ **Leaders should delegate and realize they can't do it all.**

The mind must be given relaxation—it will rise improved and sharper after a good break. Constant work gives rise to a certain kind of dullness and feebleness in the rational soul.

—Seneca, Roman Stoic philosopher, 4 BC–65 AD

BALANCE

Do you want to be really happy? You can begin by being appreciative of who you are and what you've got. Do you want to be really miserable? You can begin by being discontented.
—Benjamin Hoff, *The Tao of Pooh*

Balance: mental or emotional stability

I'm reminded of Bob Dylan's lyrics from his 1967 hit song "All Along the Watchtower," "'There must be some way out of here,' said the Joker to the Thief, 'there's too much confusion, I can't get no relief.'"

It's been said that we live in a time-starved era. Is our twenty-four seven, social media–crazed culture eating us alive or setting us free? How do we avoid "I can't get no relief?" Do we need to slow down or harness the power of speed?

Yes, the world we live in, often called Earth Incorporated, can be very confusing. Add to that volatility, complexity, uncertainty, ambiguity, disruption, and chaos, and leaders often face a tsunami of problems to solve and dilemmas to unravel. Bold and courageous leaders are always landing in areas of considerable discomfort and that's where the best ones want to be. As the old saying goes, if it were easy, everybody would do it.

But leadership isn't easy and everybody won't do it. Mastering effective leadership in an ever-demanding world is tough, challenging, at times heart breaking, and at other times exhilarating. Requiring a commitment to thrive in complexity, to build exceptional leadership teams, to motivate and not manipulate, to lead through both humility and strength, to measure success by how you affect people, realizing that everybody you lead is important—this is not for the timid, and strength requires rest and reflection.

Catch a Breath

Executive leadership coach and prolific author Robin Sharma writes:

> Retreat from the world (at least more often) and find that place of creativity, courage and serenity that sits at the root of every soul...reorder your days to clear out complexity, remove toxic negativity and release all mediocrity. You become your ecosystem. Purify your environment and your positivity and performance will rise.

Consider the following from centuries ago:

We all rush through life torn between a desire for the future and a weariness of the present...something new always comes along to keep the occupied busy. Hope begets more hope, ambition more ambition.

> **Instead of finding a new purpose, the busy just change the nature of whatever it is that preoccupies them.**
> —Seneca, Roman philosopher and statesman, 4 BC–AD 65, author of *On the Shortness of Life*

Embracing chaos in today's world, at times, seems mind-altering. It's a whirlwind of managing your work and managing your life. Happiness is certainly a part of leading a balanced life, and we'd all like to be happy, no question.

From scholar Edith Hall's new book, *Aristotle's Way: How Ancient Wisdom Can Change Your Life*, we read, "We become happy through finding a purpose, realizing our potential, and modifying our behavior to become the best version of ourselves."

Two thousand years ago, Aristotle, often referred to as the father of Western philosophy, wrote a book on happiness, telling its readers that happiness was available to everyone, if only they would make it a consistent focus. Author Hall goes on to write:

> The basic premise of Aristotle's notion of happiness is wonderfully simple and democratic: everyone can *decide* to be happy. After a certain amount of time, acting rightly becomes ingrained as a habit, so you feel good about yourself, and the resulting state of mind is one of *eudaimonia*, Aristotle's word for happiness.

So, while a life of focused leadership, one of true servant leadership, may be a daunting one, it can also bring immense joy and happiness.

Much of today's lifestyle is becoming increasingly sedentary and stressful and we wish to be filled with a certain amount of *joie de vivre* (joy of living). The human body's daily biorhythms need to be in balance to give the big energy that leaders require. Leaders need to be dynamically resilient in the face of mental, physical, and emotional challenges in order to achieve desired success. Leaders have to adjust and reset very quickly. As the noted Indian-born American author and alternative medicine advocate Deepak Chopra writes:

> Our inner awareness is a stable centering power within us that is also infinitely flexible and adaptable. This perfect integration of stability and adaptability of consciousness is what gives us the dynamic resilience we need to thrive amid the demands of our daily lives.

The obvious message becomes one of self-care. This in turn becomes one of a leader's top priorities. Leaders can't afford to give into distractions, social conformity, and someone else's perception. They can't worry about outside expectations. Leaders will seek to thrive in the present moment, and to do so, they will focus on their own well-being and eliminate negativity and empty distractions. To a large extent, leaders will find well-being through enhanced self-awareness.

Leaders know that they can create their happiness by paying attention to the life they want to live. Again, as Chopra writes:

> As we move through life, we adopt dysfunctional habits, beliefs and assumptions that deplete our energy and take us out of the now. If we make self-care a priority, we can easily replace dysfunctional habits with energy inducing habits.

Leadership can be a very lonely walk at times. The responsibilities, whether real or self-imposed, can weigh heavy. People are depending on you, people are waiting to hear from you, people are ready to follow you. Make a mistake and some people will jump all over you. Do a great job, and some people will say it really was no big deal. Yeah, you can't please all the people all the time. And good leaders know they can't run a perpetual popularity contest. As the University of Alabama's ultrasuccessful football coach, Nick Saban, says, "If you want to please people don't be a leader, go sell ice cream."

Finding a healthy balance in a life of dynamic leadership can be challenging but need not be out of reach. Balance will require reflection, introspection, self-belief, and discipline. You might remember what Ferris Bueller said in the 1986 comedy *Ferris Bueller's Day Off*, "Life moves pretty fast. If you don't stop and look around once in a while, you might miss it."

Keep a Sense of Humor

Life is serious, grades are important, parents expect a lot, teachers are demanding, and friends are sometimes not too friendly. And if you have a part-time job or working full-time in today's brutal economy, the stress level can be all-consuming.

Every successful leader, really successful leader, has a great sense of humor. It lowers blood pressure, it makes you feel good, and it relaxes you. Laughter is the body's natural medicine. This isn't hard. It's an awareness thing. Just think about it. And laugh some more.

Balance Your Technology

Recent research has revealed a dark side to a lot of the technology we use today. Maryellen Pachler, a Yale University-trained nurse practitioner who specializes in the treatment of adolescent anxiety disorders, says the glamor and gleam of social media is also fueling a rise in teen anxiety. "It can be hard to separate what you see on social media from real life." Effective leaders bury the cell phone as much as possible. They know it can be a very unwanted distraction on any given day.

Be Aware of Your Happiness

> **Every little thing is sent for something, and in that thing, there should be happiness and the power to make happy...this was the wish of the Grandfathers of the World.**
> —Black Elk, Oglala Sioux holy man and warrior, 1863–1950, from the book *Black Elk Speaks.*

Don't take being happy for granted. Don't rely on the accumulation of material things to make you happy, although it's normal to be happy with material items. Just take some time out to think about your happiness, the people and things in your life that bring you joy. Slow down and think about things and events in your life, big or small, and the people in your life, old or young, that bring you happiness.

> **Realize deeply that the present moment is all you ever have.**
> —Eckhart Tolle

Think about rewiring your brain by practicing deliberate gratitude. Take the time to value what you really have. Value your work, your health, your family, and your friends. Try keeping a gratitude journal. Write about the small moments for which you are seriously grateful. Experts tell us this can increase both our physical and mental well-being.

The World Keeps Spinning

I don't have to tell you how connected we all are, twenty-four seven. Text messaging, emails, cell phones, Twitter, Facebook, Snapchat, TikTok, and Instagram all contribute to individual overload on top of an already demanding school, business, family, and personal agenda. Your world, our world, is becoming more complex every year. We are constantly challenged to do things faster than before. It truly is the age of speed. Work quickly, work fast, get a lot done right away. Master technology and do it faster this year than last (or faster this *month* than last).

And we have already mentioned the concept of the technology paradox and the potential dangers therein. Many of you are simply wasting mental muscle by spending large amounts of time surfing totally useless information. You're crowding an extraordinary brain with needless information. This is not what exceptional leaders do.

In addition, the chaotic business world you may have already landed in, or the one you will someday face, is seemingly a heart attack looking for a place to happen. It can be frighteningly brutal. Here are a few US business facts from recent years:

> ➤ The American middle class has been shrinking as the wealth gap accelerates.

➢ One business school survey reported only 30 percent of Americans have a job they truly love.

➢ While corporate profits soar in many sectors, wage stagnation still looms large, despite the 2018 tax cut (which actually benefited larger corporations and the very wealthy).

➢ Advances in robotics and AI (artificial intelligence) have been significant, but finding the trained people to fill those job openings continues to lag demand.

➢ Americans report they are constantly under "extreme stress" as the 2020–21 COVID-19 pandemic has resulted in unprecedented business closings and job loss for millions.

The long-term effects of the COVID-19 pandemic on both business and education have yet to be seen, but suffice it to say, the impact will profoundly alter the way we learn and conduct business for years to come. The ensuing leadership challenges will demand extraordinary intellect, courage, bravery, resilience, perseverance, and drive.

But remember, there is always opportunity in adversity, and scarcity creates value. Yes, the above business facts are something to be concerned about as you begin to look ahead, but if you learn to work smart, if you master the leadership attributes you're reading about, you can move over and around a number of career difficulties that stymie most people.

Challenges All Around

The challenge for all of us collectively, really, is to make a conscious effort to lead a balanced life as best we can. Leaders must establish a set of *core values* that they will not compromise, despite the never-ending pressures to do so. We all must continue to reassess our lives, take another look, do a gut check, ask the tough questions. Am I in balance? Am I happy? Am I providing good leadership to my friends, family, school, job, team, and the like? Am I getting enough down time? Do I know how to relax amid the fast pace demands I encounter daily? Am I laughing every day?

Our world isn't likely to slow down anytime soon, if at all. You will have to take charge of finding some measure of balance in your life. Don't wait for someone else. You can make it happen by keeping in mind some of the points just mentioned.

And again, are you happy? Remember the little book, *The Tao of Pooh*, and be appreciative of what you have. Keep a winning attitude and find happiness and thankfulness in your daily life. It's all around you.

Balance and happiness go together. Have one, you're likely to have the other. Have both and you increase your chances of becoming a very good leader.

I like the following passages. Read and reflect.

> **Love your life, perfect your life, beautify all things in your life. Seek to make your life long and its purpose in the service of your people. Always give a word or sign of salute when meeting or passing a friend, even a stranger, when in a lonely place. Show respect to all people and grovel to none.**
> —Tecumseh, Native American Shawnee Chief, 1768–1813

Kind words can be short and easy to speak, but their echoes are truly endless.
—Mother Teresa, twentieth-century Albanian-Indian Roman Catholic nun, 1997 Nobel Peace Prize recipient

Being grateful, even when facing added stress and tension, can ease your discomfort and improve your life.
—Aaron Jordan, associate professor at the Centre for Positive Psychology at Melbourne Graduate School of Education, The University of Melbourne, Australia

When you are distressed by an external thing, it's not the thing itself that troubles you, but only your judgement of it. And you can wipe this out at a moment's notice.
—Marcus Aurelius, *Meditations*, Roman emperor and philosopher, 121–180 AD

Yesterday's the past, tomorrow's the future, but today is a gift. That's why it's called the present. This present is in our possession— but it has an expiration date, a quickly approaching one. If you enjoy all of it, it will be enough. It can last a whole lifetime.
—Ryan Holiday and Stephen Hanselman, *The Daily Stoic*

> **They do not grieve over the past,**
> **Nor do they yearn for the future.**
> **They live only in the present.**
> **That is why their faces are so calm.**
> —Samyutta Nikaya, Indian Buddhism, fifth century
> BC

Finding balance in a chaotic world will not be easy. Think about where you are now, where you want to go and how you will get there. And remember, we don't plan to fail, we just fail to plan. So be very careful, it's been said that the road to exhaustion is often paved with good intentions.

> **In the West, we are very goal oriented. We**
> **know where we want to go, and we are very**
> **directed in getting there. This may be useful,**
> **but often we forget to enjoy ourselves along**
> **the route.**
> —Thich Nhat Hanh, *Peace is Every Step,* Buddhist Monk,
> 1967 Nobel Peace Prize nominee

Making a Difference: Army First Lt. Brian Brennan

In 2008 twenty-five-year-old Lt. Brennan was a patrol leader in the 101st Airborne Division serving in Afghanistan. A roadside bomb killed three of Lt. Brennan's fellow soldiers while seriously injuring him. To say Lt. Brennan was seriously injured is putting it mildly.

Lt. Brennan suffered acute brain injury, collapsed lungs, internal bleeding, ruptured spleen, multiple compound fractures of both arms, and the amputation of both legs. On a scale of one to ten, with the most serious injuries being a one, doctors listed

Lt. Brennan's injuries as a one. Lt. Brennan remained in a coma until General David Petraeus visited him one day, whispered the regiment nickname in his ear, and watched in amazement as Lt. Brennan suddenly came out of his coma.

Awarded New Jersey's first Hall of Fame Unsung Heroes Award in 2009, Lt. Brennan said, "I won't be happy until I'm able to do everything I did when I had legs. I can't go back to combat because it's not ideal for me to go back. So, my mission is to help other soldiers."

Having suffered so much, Lt. Brennan put his priorities toward helping others, and in so doing, he led by example. Imagine what it took for Lt. Brennan to find balance in his "new" life. But he did it. He's the perfect example of servant leadership and finding balance in life, obstacles notwithstanding.

Leadership lessons learned: winning attitude, focus, overcoming obstacles, serving others, and finding balance.

Balance Key Points

> ➢ **Be grateful for all that you have.**

> ➢ **Find time to reflect on what you're involved in.**

> ➢ **Look for periods of solitude, find some quiet time.**

> ➢ **Be joyful; look for happiness in yourself and others.**

> ➢ **Keep a sense of humor and laugh a lot, but not at the expense of others.**

➤ **Live in the present, and follow the example of Lt. Brennan.**

Leadership Insights

➤ **The world is now dominated by problems that can't be solved and won't go away, known as dilemmas.**

➤ **Top leaders will be occupied mostly with dilemmas and may rarely get the satisfaction of solving a problem.**

➤ **Select characteristics of dilemmas are that they are confusing, complex, puzzling, recurrent, unsolvable, threatening, and potentially positive.**

➤ **An example of a flipped dilemma is that now Harvard Medical School is linked to rural Cambodia, and with a blink they can be connected.**

➤ **Leaders should realize the need to be awkward, brave, and courageous.**

Instead of challenging yourself to think outside the box, why not ask why you're in a box to begin with?

WILLIAM R. MCKENZIE, JR.

In a recent survey, 1500 CEOs were asked
to name their challenges and strategies to
address them. They named two:
- escalating complexity
- building the creative capacity in leadership
to deal with it

CREATIVE DISRUPTION

Every day, and on some days every hour, you in some way need to break set–take a different perspective, challenge the status quo, ask a different kind of question, see the world another way, and help yourself and your colleagues ask, "How would we really like it–how do we really need to have it?"
—Lynch and Kordis, *Strategy of the Dolphin, Scoring a Win in a Chaotic World*

Creative: imaginative, ingenious, innovative, original

Disruption: breaking apart, rupture, interruption of the normal course

By all accounts we're in a digital age of rapidly accelerating technology, and as this technology begins to rearrange a yo-yo economy, business leaders, who can self-destruct their organizations only to reinvent them quickly, may have the secret to economic longevity. As leadership guru Peter Drucker expressed,

> If leaders are unable to slough off yesterday, to abandon yesterday, they simply will not be able to create tomorrow.

Uber, Grubhub, TaskRabbit, Airbnb, Zwift, Lyft, WeWork, SpaceX, Stripe, JUUL Labs, DoorDash, Samumed, Infor, Coinbase, Instacart, UiPath, Tanium, Magic Leap, Stitch Fix, and on and on, creative disruptors in some form and a few unicorns (a startup company with a valuation in excess of $1 billion) are driving much of the accelerating technology pace today. It's a fasten-your-seat-belt economy for both workers and leaders, as what we see today may be gone, literally, tomorrow. This big-bang disruption phenomena will deliver complex challenges for serious leaders to navigate and thrive within.

In their 2020 insightful book *The Future Is Faster Than You Think: How Converging Technologies Are Transforming Business, Industries, and Our Lives,* authors Peter Diamandis and Steven Kotler offer the following introduction:

> Technology is accelerating far more quickly than anyone could have imagined. During the next decade, we will experience more upheaval and create more wealth than we have in the past hundred years. What happens as AI, robotics, virtual reality, digital biology and sensors crash into 3D printing, blockchain and global gigabit networks?

Disruption and the resulting chaos will become the new norm for tomorrow's leaders. Period.

Amazon, the company we can't seem to live without, is said to be "always disrupting." It annihilates and reformulates almost everything it targets. They disrupted freestanding book stores years ago, only to disrupt their own books-via-mail model by creating their Kindle e-books. Their latest disruptor is Alexa, the voice assistant that reminds us of tasks we can't remember. In 2019 Amazon became the second company to reach $1 trillion in market value (the first was Apple) and CEO Jeff Bezos has said, "We didn't ascend from our hunter-gatherer days by being satisfied."

Amazon is but one example of the path many ultrasuccessful businesses are following in our rapidly advancing digital world. The pace and complexity are causing business leaders to question past beliefs on how best to confront new markets and ever-evolving technologies. This new digital age is disrupting both old and new thoughts about business transformation and leadership. As Larry Downes and Paul Nunes wrote in their somewhat prophetic 2014 book, *Big Bang Disruption*: *Strategy in the Age of Devastating Disruption*,

> It used to take years or even decades for disruptive innovations to dethrone dominant products and services. But now any business can be devastated virtually overnight by something better and cheaper.

It has now become obvious that the nature of innovation has changed and continues to do so. Faster, more disruptive, increasingly more complex, stimulating market volatility, creating enormous wealth, and often displacing workers—it's the chaotic world we find ourselves in every day.

Creative disruption is fast becoming the new norm. The challenge for new leadership is both exciting and formidable.

Fewer jobs, more machines, in the pandemic economy, humans are being left behind.
—Alana Semuels, *Time* Magazine, August 2020

> **Leaders must be focused on cultivating thriving cultures of internal mobility, prioritizing continuous learning and delivering robust benefits to support workers.**
> —Prudential Vice Chairman Rob Falzon, Forbes 2021

In many business sectors there is no more status quo. The way things are can disappear in a blink. Most people don't like change, they look for safety, they focus on easy, and that group will be destined to either mediocrity or oblivion. The options for bold leadership are simple: choose to either survive or thrive, choose to be either boring or remarkable. People who don't ask the big questions, the hard questions, are in the majority today, but they're not in demand. Change requires bravery; managing doesn't. Research reveals that in a highly competitive world most people quit, move to the sidelines, underperform, and settle for average. But adversity can be a leader's ally, and we know that scarcity creates value.

The new economy, the accelerating and disruptive pace, is creating enormous opportunity for bold and courageous leaders, those willing to embrace a high degree of discomfort to do their best work, those who realize that the more you learn the more you achieve.

In 1989, Charles Handy, a visiting professor at The London Business School, published a book titled *The Age of Unreason,* in which he attempted to outline a new way of thinking that would better equip business and schools to deal with what he saw as massive change coming in the twenty-first century. Professor Handy knew that the new economy would place more demand on cerebral skills and less on the manual ones. This brain work is now responsible for more than 80 percent of all jobs in the US.

Leading Through Chaos

Jenn Lofgren, founder of Incito Leadership, has defined chaos as a "space of complete disorder and confusion." It's easy for leaders to get caught up in the high adrenaline rush of quickly moving issues and mounting challenges. For leaders to effectively navigate this complex environment, Ms. Lofgren offers the following seven critical leadership skills to guide leaders through chaos:

- ➢ **Trust**: trust yourself, your team, and others involved in the challenge.

- ➢ **Help**: ask for help, early and often, and don't be shy—no need to be the hero.

- ➢ **Decisions**: make decisions quickly and with serious thought. Chaos demands that you continue to move forward and make timely decisions for yourself and your team.

- ➢ **Gut instinct**: don't overlook this one, and know that trusting your intuition is often better than evidence-based decisions.

- ➢ **Break**: take a break, step away for a few minutes or longer, and look for mental clarity.

- ➢ **Eat/sleep**: chaos often takes your attention away from personal needs, and it is very easy to overlook the importance of eating and sleeping with some degree of regularity amid the chaos. Do not sacrifice eating healthy and often, and a ninety-minute nap can do wonders.

> **Composure**: keep this at all costs and do not sacrifice it; your team will need to see you set the example in this time of great disorder.

Remember, chaos may not always be about a mounting crisis, it may be about things both good and bad, and successful leaders must learn how to think and communicate clearly, stay calm, and guide their teams effectively.

Becoming Disruptive

In the business world there's a term called *dominant logic*. It refers to people who possess deeply held assumptions about the world. The inference is that for these people to be successful, they'll have to learn to be more open to thinking differently, to change their *deeply held assumptions* and see the world as it is, a rapidly changing mass of people and information.

Deeply held assumptions may get in the way of your ability to create necessary change, of your ability to break the status quo, of your ability to take risks and think creatively and disruptively.

Tackling risk sometimes requires a *disruptive* approach. It demands a *different* look at approaching the dilemma before you. You might need to find *options* to the risks you're facing and this might require a more *creative* thought process.

Terms like *unreasonable, different, creative,* and *disruptive* illustrate both the need and the value of thinking in nontraditional ways to manage the risks that will invariably come your way in the business world. As an effective leader navigating incoming chaos, the decisions you will face, the risks you will need to manage, the complexity of challenges that arrive, will be significant if not extraordinary. Some may be answered with little thought or effort at all. Others will demand that you become creatively disruptive in thought and problem-solving. Serious leaders will often need to

> ➤ see the world in a different way,
> ➤ break set, trash the status quo,
> ➤ ask the *big* questions, ask the *hard* questions,
> ➤ forget dominant logic, understand the speed of technology and change, and
> ➤ become productively and creatively disruptive—break rules where necessary.

Take an in-depth look at companies like Bumble, CRISPR, Uber, Netflix, PARSLEY, and Cirque du Soleil to see the impact of creative disruption.

"We just seem to thrive on adversity."
—Seven-time NASCAR Cup champion Jimmie Johnson, founder of the Jimmie Johnson Foundation with an emphasis on K–12 education

Business Is Changing

Ori Brafman and Rod Beckstrom, authors of *The Starfish and the Spider*: *The Unstoppable Power of Leaderless Organizations,* argue that some very successful organizations are like starfish. Cut off a leg and it grows a new leg, one that can grow into a new starfish. But cut off a spider's head and it dies. The traditional spider-like organizations are top-down in structure while starfish organizations are changing the look of businesses all around the world. Here, they lay it out quite simply:

> Strarfish systems are wonderful incubators for creative, destructive, innovative, or crazy ideas.

Anything goes. Good ideas will attract more people, and in a circle, they'll execute a plan. Institute
order and rigid structure, and while you may
achieve standardization, you'll also squelch creativity. **While creativity is valuable**, **learning to accept chaos is a must**.

They go on to say:

This type of leadership is not ideal for all situations. **Catalysts are bound to rock the boat**.
They are much better at being agents of change
than guardians of tradition. Catalysts do well in
situations that call for radical change and creative
thinking. They bring innovation, but they're also
likely to create a certain amount of chaos and ambiguity. Put them into a structured environment,
and they might suffocate. **But let them dream
and they'll thrive**.

Lifelong, full-time jobs have virtually disappeared. Work is
becoming increasingly more complex, with uncertainty and volatility the norm. Global expansion is demanding a new set of skills.
Your capacity to learn and adapt, connect with others (networking)
and show some measure of resilience will be required. Experts
project you'll change jobs seven to ten times over the course of
your working career and that's a guess at best. Chaos doesn't
always lead to reliable predictions.

As a bold and effective leader, you will, at times, have to become *unreasonable* and *productively disruptive*. To have any real chance
at success in today's chaotic world, you must target to become the
best leader you can possibly be. Leadership is fast approaching

the realm of healthy survival. It's no longer a business luxury. It's not a spectator sport. And if you have critics, and it's a guarantee that you will, then you must be doing something(s) right.

What if I told you that everything you know is wrong?

My point would be, your assumptions about the world may need creative change to move successfully forward.

Many successful business leaders today are changing their business models to focus on the "why" of their business, not the "what." Customers now want to know why your business does what it does and are willing to pay for that why factor. They place less emphasis (and value) on what your business does.

Do you know why you do what you do? Wouldn't you want to hire people who believe in why you do what you do? Martin Luther King Jr. said, "I have a dream," not "I have a plan."

In Simon Sinek's groundbreaking book, *Start With Why: How Great Leaders Inspire Everyone to Take Action*, he writes:

> There are leaders and there are those that lead. Leaders hold a position of power or influence. Those who lead inspire us. Whether individuals or organizations, we follow those who lead not because we have to, but because we want to. We follow those who lead not for them, but for ourselves.
>
> We are drawn to leaders and organizations that are good at communicating what they believe. The role of a leader is not to come up with all the great ideas. The role of a leader is to create an environment in which great ideas can happen.

As today's leaders plow ahead and embrace the chaos, keeping a focus on the *why* of what they represent and do will be critical to both personal and team success.

A New Circus, New Tunes, New Cars, New Threads

Case in point is the world-renowned *Cirque du Soleil* (Circus under the Sun). It's somewhat of a business paradox, in that it's a circus, but certainly not a traditional circus, no animal acts but a lot of people. People are the circus, not the animals. Yet, the Cirque model is a more profitable and a more sustainable model over time, one that continues to deliver circus-style entertainment. But, without breaking with past circus assumptions, this highly creative and extremely popular venue would not have evolved. Thinking differently, asking out-of-the-box questions, and looking to create meaningful change was critical to success. The Cirque du Soleil team was most definitely not thinking status quo and their result was a *creative disruption* of the iconic big tent model.

Being creatively disruptive in today's climate means embracing change and bucking the status quo. It's often referred to as *upside down thinking* or thinking *outside of the box*. (Of course, the big question is, why are you in a box to begin with?) It gets back to what leaders have to do to become effective—thinking differently, taking creative approaches to solve problems, work these changes through people, not by themselves; more servant leadership, more we, and less me.

Sometimes you just have to break the rules, as alarming as that may seem. It's what leaders have to do, become creatively and productively disruptive.

Breaking rules is what happened at Apple Computer as they developed the industry changing iPod. Many Apple employees wanted no part of this project, opting out for the company to make more computers. After all, that's what Apple was known for and their success was legendary. Why change?

But another segment of Apple's employees began to look at market data, information that was telling them that people wanted mobile computing. In what has since been called market bravery, Apple took the leap and managed the risk to apply their computer expertise to a new business model.

The iPod was born and followed by the extraordinary iPhone, great examples of being *creatively disruptive* to develop new game-changing technology. Apple leaders lead their teams through times of challenging chaos, finding ways to thrive, not just survive.

Breaking rules is what happened at Ford Motor Company in 2008. Rather than accept government bailout monies to combat the economic disaster facing many large American corporations at that time, Ford charted its own path to success by listening to its customers and learning from past mistakes. Ford began to think differently. How could they make new hybrid cars, how could they radically improve gas mileage, how could they run their manufacturing plants more cost effectively, how could they keep thousands of employees on the payroll and save their families the trauma of lost jobs?

Ford hired a *nonindustry* executive to lead the company, an executive from Boeing Corporation, a maker of airplanes. In 2011 Ford achieved record profits. Who was thinking differently? Who was unreasonable? Who was creatively disruptive?

Thinking differently is what led young entrepreneur Pharrell Williams to team up with Tyson Toussant at Bionic Yarns to create an eco-friendly apparel company. Creating premium yarns from recycled plastic beverage bottles, Bionic Yarns is making a wide variety of consumer products, ranging from backpacks to hand-bags to denim wear to outdoor furnishings, all environmentally friendly, and equally sustainable.

Did these guys rely on traditional business thinking to create a new market? Were their strategic planning days low key and easy? Did they follow tried and true manufacturing operations? How many *big* questions did they ask? How many dead-ins did they encounter? How many times were they told to give up on the goal? How did they successfully move through all the naysayers? Listening to the way things are—no. Embracing the creative chaos of a *big* idea—most definitely.

Work to change the status quo, work to make meaningful change, work at becoming a creative disruptor to lead your teams to new economic models. This is what effective leaders do as they work through chaos.

Remember, those who *do not ask the hard questions* are in today's majority, but they are not in demand. Scarcity creates value. Be disruptive, embrace the chaos and enjoy the journey!

A recent *Harvard Business Review* article highlighted the need for successful leaders to embrace disrupting themselves as they moved along their leadership journey. Disrupters look for needs in the market that are not being met. So, if you've reached a plateau in life or business/career pursuit, you might want to look at what you do well that most others can't, don't, or will not do.

It's estimated that 70 percent of all successful business ventures end up with a strategy different from the one initially outlined. That magnitude and complexity of change requires strong and resourceful leadership and leaders must realize the status quo usually has a powerful undertow. Resistance to change can be expected.

Leading Dynamic Change Successfully

The Center for Creative Leadership's Dr. Cheng Zhu has outlined what her research indicates are the top three challenges facing leaders as they prepare to lead their teams through tremendous chaos and change. How do they overcome the overwhelming resistance to change?

One, leaders must *communicate* clearly and effectively. Where are we going? What's our purpose? Why is change necessary? What's our game plan? How will we know when we're successful?

Two, leaders must focus on creating meaningful *alignments* and seek to establish strategic priorities. Who will the team(s) be interacting with? Why? What are their skill sets and why are they important to our strategy? Are all of our roles clearly defined?

Three, leaders must maintain honest *commitment* to their teams, to the targeted challenges and to themselves. Establishing an atmosphere of mutual trust and accountability is paramount to success. The importance of strong emotional intelligence, a leader's ability to make the necessary connection effectively and honestly with team members, should not be overlooked.

As Jim Collins, the author of the intensely researched leadership book, *Good to Great*, writes,

> You can either follow a paint-by-numbers-kit approach to life and do what everybody thinks you should do and stay within the accepted lines, or you can decide you want to create a masterpiece and start with a blank canvas.

Another perspective comes from the 2019 book by Abbosh, Nunes and Downes titled, *Pivot to the Future: Discovering Value and Creating Growth in a Disrupted World*. With a focus on the rapidly changing need for different leadership styles, they write,

Accepting the need for different kinds of leadership can be one of the hardest things for managers in today's business, especially when their own style doesn't fit with their companies' requirements in the new…There is an inherent trade-off between leaders focused on business creation (entrepreneurs) versus leaders focused on business running (operators). In an environment characterized by continual disruption, you'll need both…Pivoting to the future can only happen if leaders are prepared to leave the safe harbor of today. And that takes courage.

Remember, dismiss bad air, negativity and the eventual critics and complainers. Believe in yourself and your leadership ability. Understand that immersive learning makes you a game-changer. Focus on what it takes to be a creative disruptor in your field and embrace the challenges of dynamic leadership in a chaotic world, and don't forget to enjoy the journey!

He taught us to think differently and to have the courage to change, often in unconventional ways, always acting with a sense of responsibility for the companies and their people.
—John Elkann, Fiat automotive heir, speaking on the death of Chrysler CEO Sergio Marchionne in July 2018

Making a Difference: Marny Xiong

Like most high-impact leaders, Marny Xiong had laser focus, passion and a moral compass pointing her to a life of servant leadership. Driven? Absolutely. Brave? Unmistakable. Big emotional IQ? Without a doubt.

Marny was one of eight children born to Hmong parents in 1989, parents who came to St. Paul, Minnesota from Laos as part of a resettlement program for families of Hmong soldiers who had aided the CIA in Laos during the Vietnam War. Her family lived in public housing, Marny was the fourth of eight children, and life was tough for a large family in a strange land.

Attending St. Paul public schools, by the time Marny was in high school she had a passion for learning and leadership. Graduating from the University of Minnesota at Duluth in 2012 with an interest in law and politics, she went to work at the Food Group, a local antihunger organization. From there she joined Take Action Minnesota, a community organizing group. A committed activist, she worked on campaigns to raise the minimum wage and to oppose state amendments requiring voter ID and banning same-sex marriage.

Running for the St. Paul School Board in 2017, she would become the youngest school board chairman in its history. School board Vice-Chair Jeanelle Foster said, "Marny was always really strong and vocal. I call her my badass!"

When her father began having breathing difficulties one day, she drove him to the local hospital. There, both father and daughter were diagnosed with COVID-19. Her father survived, but Marny never came off the ventilator, passing away on June 7, 2020 at the age of thirty-one.

Marny's sister, Amee, said, "She had so many dreams and goals. We could have reached a lot of people."

In the greater leadership world Marny Xiong stands out as a game-changer. She made good things happen for a lot of people. She was brave, courageous, empathetic, kind and a problem solver. Make no mistake, the world needs more Marny Xiongs.

Leadership lessons learned: winning attitude, passion, focus, serving others, dreaming big, courage

Select Disruptive Leaders Today

Jon Bon Jovi

➢ Hall of Fame rock musician

➢ Established the JBJ Soul Kitchen for Community Dining with Dignity to serve those experiencing food hardship

➢ Since beginning in 2011, more than 127,000 meals have been served, 51 percent of customers earned meals by volunteering and 49 percent paid for meals with donations

➢ With an estimated net worth of $400 million, Jon has been washing dishes during the COVID-19 pandemic

Nemonte Nenquimo

➢ President of Waorani of Pastaza

➢ Cofounder of Ceibo Alliance

➢ Won a major lawsuit protecting the Waorani tribe's Amazon lands in Ecuador from being devoured by big oil companies

Maya Moore

> ➤ Basketball WNBA champion, Olympic gold medalist

> ➤ *Sports Illustrated* calls her the "greatest winner in the history of women's basketball"

> ➤ She left the WNBA in 2019 to pursue criminal justice reform

> ➤ She won the release of Jonathan Irons who spent twenty years in prison following a wrongful conviction

Nathan Law

> ➤ Prodemocracy activist who led the opposition to communist Beijing's suppression of Hong Kong

> ➤ The youngest lawmaker elected to Hong Kong's city legislature

> ➤ Driven into exile for defending people's democratic rights

Eric Yuan

> ➤ Founded Zoom, the one click videoconferencing software company

➤ Zoom has become the backbone of business team meetings, weddings, and classroom learnings for millions of students during the COVID-19 pandemic

➤ Admired by 98 percent of his employees, his leadership style has been described as humble.

Jacinda Arden

➤ Fortieth Prime Minister of New Zealand who worked in a New York soup kitchen feeding the poor and hungry after university graduation

➤ The world's youngest head of government at age thirty-seven in 2017

➤ The world's second-youngest elected head of government to give birth while in office in 2018

➤ In 2019 after fifty-one people were killed in two mosques in Christchurch, she led a successful ban on assault rifles in New Zealand and personally visited the Muslim relatives of those murdered

Gisele Barreto Fetterman

➤ Thirty-nine-year-old Second Lady of Pennsylvania, wife of the Lieutenant Governor

> ➤ Brazilian American activist, a former undocumented immigrant

> ➤ Cofounder of 412 Food Rescue, a nonprofit organization focused on combating food insecurity and providing nutritional resources

> ➤ Named the "Best Activist" and the emcee of World Refugee Day in 2018

Creative Disruption Key Points

> ➤ **Begin to think creatively, and ask the *big* questions.**

> ➤ **Look for ways to create meaningful and dynamic change.**

> ➤ **Work to effectively break the status quo.**

> ➤ **Always ask, "Is there a better way?"**

> ➤ **Pay little or no attention to your critics.**

> ➤ **Focus on immersive learning and emotional intelligence.**

Leadership Insights

> ➤ Leaders always remember the importance of humility and gratitude.

> ➤ Leadership is often defined as someone who has only one thing, followers.

> ➤ Big leaders choose motivation and inspiration over manipulation.

> ➤ Catalytic leaders challenge the status quo, they always ask *why?*

> ➤ Leaders should be the Navy SEALs of the business world, taking care of their employees, their teams, their relationships.

I just want to do something meaningful.
—Usher, five-time Grammy winner, founder of the *New Look Foundation,* an organization focused on assisting economically disadvantaged youth

COMPASSION

I cursed the fact I had no shoes until I saw the man who had no feet.
—Saadi, Medieval Persian poet

Compassion: deep sympathy

The Amazing Jordan Thomas
Fifteen-year-old Jordan Thomas was enjoying a great family vacation while scuba diving off the coast of South Florida. Here's the story in his own words:

> While scuba diving in the Florida Keys, a boat propeller struck both my legs. I was sent to the Ryder Trauma Center in Miami where I underwent three surgeries, and I lost both of my legs from the calf down. I spent about two weeks in the hospital and returned home to undergo rehabilitation. My rehabilitation has been tough, but I have been given every opportunity possible.
>
> When I was in the hospital, I was really touched by the kids who would never be able to achieve their

dreams because they did not have the money to continue their recovery and rehabilitation.

Larry was one boy who had been severely burned and was recovering in the Trauma Rehabilitation Unit. He had almost no resources with which to continue his rehabilitation after discharge. To make matters worse, Larry was placed on a waiting list to go to a foster home as his parents had abandoned him. I felt great sadness about his many losses and grateful for all the loving support I have received during my recovery.

With that in mind, I have set up the *Jordan Thomas Foundation* to raise money for children with traumatic injuries who are not as fortunate as I.

Once again, in Jordan's own words, here are some of the kids his foundation has touched:

Our first beneficiary of the Jordan Thomas Foundation is named Alaina and she is now 8 years old. Alaina lives near Chattanooga and when she was 2 years old, she was in a farming accident. She lost both her legs, one above the knee and the other below the knee leading to a difficult rehabilitation. She spent several weeks at TC Thompson's Children's Hospital and her medical expenses were very high. Her family was unable to afford replacement prosthesis for those she had outgrown.

I am excited to tell you about our second beneficiary. Noah is 6 years old and an amazingly happy child despite everything he has been through. Noah was born with a serious heart defect requiring four separate surgical procedures. While recovering from his first open heart surgery at three weeks of age, Noah suffered a complication resulting in loss of blood flow to his right leg. The leg could not be saved and he underwent an amputation at the knee.

Noah has just completed his fourth and final heart surgery and has made a remarkable recovery over the past several weeks. He has been fitted with a new "leg" and a new "knee" made possible by the Jordan Thomas Foundation and generous sponsors.

Noah is filled with the joy of life despite the incredible hardships he and his family have endured. Recently, Noah asked if he could have a foot with a split toe to allow him to wear sandals like Mom and Dad. We were delighted to help and have made his life a little easier.

Leaders have and show genuine compassion for those around them.

They know that serving others has a major impact on everyone involved and beyond, close friends and strangers alike, and that compassion is the mark of a true servant leader. Jordan Thomas is a shining example *of leading with compassion.*

Why America's Top Technology Jobs Are Going to Indian Executives

This was the title of a 2015 *Wall Street Journal* article outlining the leadership success in the technology sector of our economy. While the names Nadella, Pichai, Suri, and Narayen may not be familiar names to us, the companies they run are: Microsoft, Google, Nokia, and Adobe Systems. The CEOs of some of the world's most recognizable tech companies are seen to have origins from India.

A cross-cultural study conducted by Southern New Hampshire University analyzed managers from the US and India, finding that more Indian managers scored higher in terms of meaningful leadership traits. The study went on to conclude that Indian managers are future-oriented and have a "paradoxical blend of genuine personal humility and intense professional will. These leaders achieved extraordinary results and built great organizations without much hoopla."

The big leadership takeaway? Compassion, humility, decency, and kindness are vital leadership attributes in our chaotic, volatile, complex, and sometimes very confusing world today. It's less me and more we. It's about making the all-important emotional connection with employees. It's not about running a popularity contest. It's about being a multiplier, working to elevate your teams to higher performance and motivating them with a combination of business expertise, clarity of mission, and decent leadership.

With a unique leadership perspective offered in their book titled *Leading with Soul,* authors Lee Bolman and Terrence Deal write:

> Perhaps we lost our way when we forgot that the heart of leadership lies in the *hearts* of leaders. We fooled ourselves, thinking that sheer bravado or sophisticated analytic techniques could respond to

our deepest concerns. We lost touch with a most
precious human gift—our spirit.

Someone once said that your strength is based in your humility. Think about it, seriously.

A Nigerian Story of Excellence

When you embrace and show compassion, you truly make a difference, and that's what *servant leadership* is all about. Take a look at
the story of Nnamdi Asomugha, a professional football cornerback
and native of Nigeria.

Nnamdi's parents fled the impoverished African country of
Nigeria when he was a boy. His family quickly taught him the
value of giving to those less fortunate while surrounded by the
beauty of Southern California, their newly adopted home. A
standout student-athlete in high school, Nnamdi attended the
University of California at Berkley. He graduated with a degree
in corporate finance, was a standout safety on the football team,
and was selected by the Oakland Raiders in the NFL draft.

Nnamdi quickly achieved success with the Raiders, making
the Pro Bowl team, and was so highly regarded that the Raiders
made him the highest paid defensive back in NFL history. His
reputation as a charitable giver was gaining just as much press.
Among his many compassionate efforts toward others are:

➢ Regular visits to the East Oakland Youth Development
Center to tutor inner-city youth

➢ Providing shoes and running attire to underprivileged
children

➢ Creating an Asomugha College Tour for Students, providing inner-city achieving students with free college tours to broaden their educational experience

"My experience with the Center reminded me to always have my eyes open for opportunities to give back." Nnamdi's success strategies are:

➢ Always seek opportunities to make a difference for others

➢ Nurture a spirit of giving in your children

➢ Share your abundance—whether it's your time, wisdom, or money

For all his charitable efforts in the Oakland area, Nnamdi has not forgotten his native home. He serves as the chairman for his family's charity, the Orphans and Widows in Need Foundation. The charity provides food, shelter, medicine, and scholarships to orphans and widows in Nigeria.

Indeed, Nnamdi Asomugha is a great example of leading with compassion. He could be spending his free time and considerable resources doing things more self-centered, but he chooses to lead by example.

Those who are without compassion cannot see what is seen with the eyes of compassion.
—Thich Nhat Hanh, *The Miracle of Mindfulness*

Authors Rosamund and Benjamin Zander touch on one of the deepest meanings of empathetic and compassionate leadership in their thought-provoking book, *The Art of Possibility*:

> Yet we do have the capacity to override the hidden assumptions of peril that give us the world we see. Leadership is a relationship that brings possibility to others and to the world, from any chair, from any role. This kind of leader is not necessarily the strongest member of the pack, the one best suited to fend off the enemy and gather in resources, as our old definitions of leadership sometimes had it. The "leader of possibility" invigorates the lines of affiliation and *compassion* from person to person in the face of the tyranny of fear. Any one of us can exercise this kind of leadership, whether we stand in the position of CEO or employee, citizen or elected official, teacher or student. This leader calls upon our *passion* rather than our fear. She is the relentless architect of the possibility that humans can be.

You are living in a world of finite resources. Compassion should not be one of those scarce resources. Rise above the daily chaos. You have the capacity to give and serve others for a life time. Do so wisely and become a true servant leader.

Think about what Jordan Thomas was able to do while still in high school. Think about what Nnamdi Asomugha was able to do through hard work, focus and compassion for others.

Think about what the Roman statesman and lawyer Cicero wrote in his influential philosophical work *De Officiis* (On Duties):

"Not for us are we born; our country, our friends, have a share in us."

Think about what rock musician and community leader Jon Bon Jovi has said, "If you want to feel good, then do good."

Think about what leadership expert and author Robin Sharma has said, "The most noble thing you can do is give to others. Start focusing on your higher purpose."

Think about what noted breast cancer surgeon Dr. Eleni Tousimis has said, "It's about finding happiness in helping others, creating peace within yourself and around you and finding your passion and purpose. This is what we as humans should be striving for."

Leaders should challenge themselves to embrace the chaos, go and do what others will not do, find success and happiness in areas of discomfort, and at the end of their life's journey, ask themselves the question—how many people have I helped?

Nature bids us to do well by all...Wherever there is a human being, we have an opportunity for kindness.
—Seneca, Roman Stoic philosopher, 4 BC–AD 65

Making a Difference: Taylor LeBaron

How many teenagers do you know who have written and published a book by age seventeen? How many of your friends are seriously overweight, maybe even suffering morbid obesity, have lost half their weight through focus, discipline, sense of urgency, and winning attitude? Cutting their weight in half?

That's exactly what Taylor LeBaron accomplished when, as an obese fourteen-year-old, he began a personal quest to shed 150 lbs. from his 300 lb. frame. It wouldn't be easy. His junk food cravings and no-exercise lifestyle led to taunts from other kids, like "Whoa, dude, you need a bra." Running was out of the question. He got winded just walking. Taylor was a big kid early on. By the third grade he weighed 130 lbs. when most kids were less than 100. The summer before the seventh grade, Taylor topped his grandmother's scales at 297 lbs. He knew he was in trouble.

Taylor had to wear size forty-four jeans—hard to find. Three-X t-shirts—hard to find. School desks were too small. Theme park rides had weight limits, and he easily exceeded them. Class projects like clearing a nature trail were not only embarrassing, but also physically impossible. On a class field trip to Stone Mountain, Georgia, Taylor's classmates decided to hike one of the trails. It just about killed him. He realized the extra weight was like a virus attacking a computer. Corrective measures would have to be taken.

Just after Taylor's fourteenth birthday, his grandparents gave his family a YMCA membership, a pivotal event in Taylor's quest to begin a new life. At the Y he would begin to understand the value of goal setting, becoming results-oriented, staying focused, making sacrifices, developing a sense of urgency toward his overall health, and becoming passionate about his new goals.

Taylor began a leadership quest to become a better person by developing his whole self.

As Taylor points out in his book, *Cutting Myself in Half, 150 Pounds Lost One Byte at a Time,* 9 million US teens are overweight and the problem is escalating at alarming rates. A no-exercise and junk food lifestyle is literally killing the youth of America. Says Dr. Mike Dansinger, noted nutrition expert,

> Today's teens are tomorrow's leaders. The future depends on you. The world, as well as your body, is what you make of it. You can lead or follow the pack. You can win or you can lose.

Leadership lessons learned: focus, urgency, passion, creativity, and winning attitude

Compassion Key Points

➢ **Focus on serving others.**

➢ **Be grateful for what you have.**

➢ **Become a community volunteer.**

➢ **Think about what Jordan Thomas has been able to do.**

➢ **Find a fellow classmate that could use your help.**

➢ **Pray for peace, every day.**

Leadership Insights

➢ **As economic complexity increases leaders will find themselves in a thrive versus survive mode.**

➢ **In a chaotic world, humility, compassion, and kindness are needed areas of leadership strength.**

➢ Leaders should remind themselves of the need, not the requirement, to be lifelong learners, and their business culture should reflect the same.

➢ Leaders must be aware of the pitfalls in dominant logic as they evaluate their business success and failures moving forward.

I know it's a challenge to try and ride 112 miles without the use of quads or hamstrings and then get off the bike and run a marathon, but I knew to change the perception of what someone with a disability can accomplish, finishing the Ironman under all the time cut-offs was a huge step not only for me, but for all the kids and adults who are out there dealing with limb loss and other challenges.

—Rudy Garcia Tolson, age seventeen, both legs amputated at age five, Ironman triathlon finisher and swimming world record holder

PERSEVERANCE

Be stubborn. There's a lot of people who'll say you can't do something. Just be stubborn. Do it anyway.
—Twenty-six-year-old US Army Sgt. Brendan Marrocco, having lost both legs and both arms in Iraq, the first service member to receive a double arm transplant in 2013.

Persevere: to continue a course of action in spite of difficulty, opposition, and so forth.

We hear about courageous stories all the time, stories of seemingly unbelievable accomplishment in the face of incredible odds. They're all around us, but do we really learn leadership lessons from these heroes, or do we just click onto the next tag line and miss the real meaning?

Do we really understand what it means to persevere; to, as Sgt. Marrocco said, "Just be stubborn, do it anyway"? Do we know how to overcome life's many obstacles? Do we have a strong grit factor? Do we know how to gut it out when times get tough? Are we willing to push forward, realizing that as engaged leaders we will definitely experience failure at some point and maybe more than once? Are great leaders willing to take that heat? Are you?

Bold, courageous, and effective leaders totally understand perseverance. Whatever the challenge, they embrace the chaotic moment and find a pathway forward. In the new world of big bang disruption, it's all about leaders managing their energy to thrive in high-stress environments, realizing that life just may be a series of all-out sprints where leadership purpose fuels high performance.

Great leadership isn't defined when times are good. It surfaces when it gets really hard, and courage, tenacity and resolve become the way forward.

> **The one thing I always said to my kids is—and it's the biggest thing I can instill in them—is to never give up.**
>   —Mark Cavendish, Professional Cyclist, winner of three consecutive races in 2021 after a two-year absence with a serious illness

Always Looking Up

Meaningful leadership is often about walking into areas of unknown consequences. When Sgt. Brendan Marrocco awoke in that army hospital bed and realized he had lost both arms and legs, he no doubt found himself in an unimaginable mental place. His thoughts must have been mind-numbing with fear, disbelief, shock, agony, and perhaps even a sense of hopelessness. He could have given up, right then and there, in his hospital bed, no arms, no legs. We would have understood.

No life? Give up? Self-pity? Maybe he thought about it for a moment, and we would have understood that, too. He was a soldier, he was tough, he was in combat, he knew the score. Nevertheless, losing both arms and legs wasn't something he focused on. But now it was real, someone else's nightmare was his.

> I hated not having arms. I was alright with not
> having legs. Not having arms takes so much away
> from you, even your personality. You talk with
> your hands. You do everything. When you don't
> have that, you are kind of lost for a while.

And what were the first words spoken by Sgt. Marrocco after surgery? He looked around at all the medical personnel and simply said, "I love you."

Sgt. Marrocco understands what it takes to overcome the most formidable obstacles in life. And at that moment, a very big leadership moment, he also understands the profound meaning of humility and gratitude. And he does what all great leaders do, he finds a way to renew himself in the midst of serious adversity. He finds a way to tell his team how much they mean to him, he puts a smile on his face and prepares for a new life, an exciting life, a life full of energy, and perseverance.

Army Sgt. Marrocco is only one of seven people who have received a double arm transplant and he was the first quad amputee to survive the wars in Iraq and Afghanistan. His attitude is a champion's one, his focus is laser-like, and his passion for life unquestionable. And he has already embraced that attribute that is so critical to successful leadership—perseverance. He will no doubt conquer one obstacle and then move on to the next one. That is serious leadership.

What we know about bold and effective leadership in a chaotic world, what separates the exceptional from the average, is that sooner or later, all leaders will be faced with a considerable undertow of obstacles, serious problems, or dilemmas that present seemingly no-win situations to work through.

Colleges and Universities Are Reevaluating

It's interesting to hear how some colleges and universities are now trying to measure a high school student's grit factor as part of the admission process. How tough is the student? How does the student react to obstacles encountered in life? How well does the student push through adversity to achieve an announced goal? Is he or she likely to give up early?

Colleges and universities are in the business of education, obviously. In purely financial terms this means that every space granted to an incoming freshman can be seen as a tuition paying slot. If that slot becomes vacant prior to graduation then again, in purely financial terms, its money lost by the school. Their investment in that student didn't pay off. In a world of finite resources, in a world of ever-increasing cost awareness in all business sectors, colleges, and universities want to make sure their selections will last, that every student admitted will persevere through the college experience. Empty student spaces create revenue shortfall, its money lost.

Colleges and universities today want to measure a student's mental toughness, realizing that there's more to great grades and test scores as a predictor of educational success. College is tough, some more so than others. There will be any number of leadership moments challenging students. You can step up or step out.

Talent doesn't make you "gritty," there are many talented individuals who simply do not follow through on their commitments.
—Angela Duckworth

Blind and On Top of the World—Literally

At 29,000-plus feet, Mount Everest is the tallest mountain on the planet. Temperatures down to −60°F, winds known to reach 100 miles per hour, solid rock and ice, deep ice fissures called crevasses, fall into one and you're frozen toast, snow falling year around, climbers known to die from pulmonary edema (lungs fill up with fluid) and cerebral edema (brain swells with fluid), climbers entering the death zone at 24,000 feet (so little oxygen the body begins to die little by little), and that's a normal day on the mountain. It can get worse.

Eric Weihenmayer climbed Mount Everest, summiting on May 25, 2001. Blind since early childhood, Eric rarely took no for an answer when identifying a specific challenge to attack. Adventure sports became his passion, and climbing Everest was an obvious choice for Eric.

The skill set it takes to climb high mountains is extensive— technically, physically, and mentally. Think ice climbing, big wall climbing, avalanche reading, team work versus big egos, ability to think clearly and quickly under extreme climactic conditions, serious total body coordination, a VO2 Max off the chart, and much more. It's one of the most demanding of all sports. The danger factor may be the absolute highest of all.

What Eric accomplished in 2001 is a text book example of perseverance. What Eric did on Mt. Everest is what all bold and courageous leaders do at some point on their leadership journey. They persevere through seemingly impossible odds. They tackle the toughest problems and dilemmas with warrior-type resolve. They know they will find a way to a successful solution. They're not quitters just because it would be easy to do so, and maybe even understandable if they did. Successful leaders will lead their teams to accomplish extraordinary results by embracing the chaos, working in areas of extreme discomfort because that's where they do their best work, and persevering through the tough journey.

A Future Look

While predicting the future of most anything in our world today may well be an exercise in magic, there are some givens that are easy to pinpoint, and they will require extraordinary, focused, tenacious and wise leadership to navigate successfully.

Perseverance will be an absolute key to successful leadership and there's no magic knowing that.

Bob Johansen's book, *Leaders Make the Future*, offers a deep look into what serious leaders must embrace to win in an expanding world of chaos and complexity, of confusion and uncertainty, of volatility and ambiguity. One key question for all leaders of the future is, do you want to thrive or just opt out and survive? What will it take to thrive?

> **I can accept failure; everyone fails at something. But I can't accept not trying.**
> —Michael Jordan, NBA Hall of Fame, six-time NBA champion

Some leaders today are easily overwhelmed, while others are quickly planning on how best to launch their leadership skills into an unpredictable and chaotic future. These leaders are well aware of the importance of immersive learning, a term Bob Johansen writes about extensively in his book. As Mr. Johansen outlines nine additional leadership traits thriving leaders will need for the future, the concept of serious perseverance becomes even more important. How will bold leaders master concepts like maker instinct, clarity, dilemma flipping, bioempathy, constructive depolarization, quiet transparency, rapid prototyping, smart-mob mobilization, and commons creating?

Leading in a disrupted world, where the pressure of external forces on traditional leadership will require a new leadership mindset, is likely to be both exciting and dangerous. Leaders tend to want to problem solve quickly, but new opportunities may remain unseen and added value may be missed in early problem or dilemma analysis. The stress, the physical and mental fatigue, and the challenge of *relentless perseverance* to lead, will challenge both the mindset and heartset of leaders for the future. And remember, someone once said "if it doesn't challenge you, it doesn't change you."

Bold and courageous leadership is definitely an embrace-the-chaos journey for those rising to the challenge, and that's the space where inspirational leaders find success and happiness, so enjoy the journey!

Don't forget: your leadership is defined by what and who you tolerate.

Making a Difference: Rudy Garcia Tolson

Rudy's life was a challenge from day one. Born in 1988 with rare multiple birth defects that included crippling Pterygium Syndrome, a club foot, webbed fingers and a cleft lip and palate, who would have thought that this child would one day set world swimming records and finish a full Ironman triathlon?

By age five, Rudy had endured fifteen operations, was confined to a wheelchair and had little hope of playing with friends, let alone participating in sports of any kind. That's when Rudy asked his parents to approve a double leg amputation. He was just too tired of the wheelchair. He wanted another chance at life even it meant having no legs. So, at age five, Rudy had both legs amputated above the knee.

"For me, having my legs amputated at age 5 was the best thing that ever happened. After the amputation a whole world of activities opened for me and today, I'm a surfer, a skateboarder, runner, cyclist, swimmer, triathlete and Ironman finisher. Sport is a great equalizer."

Indeed, it is. Rudy competed in the 2004 Athens Paralympic Games where, at age sixteen, he set a new world record in the 200-meter individual medley swim event in his class. In 2008 at the Beijing Paralympics he once again set a new world record in the 200-meter IM. And in 2009, at age 21, Rudy completed the Arizona Ironman in sixteen hours and six minutes.

Rudy has helped raise over $6 million for the Challenged Athlete Foundation and has received numerous awards for his inspiration and leadership, including the Arete Courage in Sports Award and the Casey Martin Award from Nike.

To say that Rudy has shown perseverance in the face of so many life challenges doesn't do justice. Rudy has truly been a *servant leader, taking risks, pushing limits, staying focused, competing with passion and an inexhaustible winning attitude.*

"To lead by example and show others that the sky is the limit motivates me to continue to push boundaries."

Without question, Rudy has embraced chaos and is enjoying the journey!

Leadership lessons learned: passion, attitude, perseverance, focus, urgency

Perseverance Key Points

- ➤ Remember the importance of a winning attitude—it gets you through tough times.

- ➤ Don't forget the power of staying focused—move through distractions.

- ➤ Look for someone you know who has met an extreme challenge with success—how did they do it?

- ➤ Find a classmate who is struggling with a major problem—see if you can be of assistance.

- ➤ Don't forget the life story of Rudy Garcia Tolson and others like him.

Leadership Insights

- ➤ High-impact leaders realize that good and fast is often better than slow and perfect.

- ➤ Effective leaders know the importance of self-awareness and its evolving components—wisdom, identity, reputation, and brand.

- ➤ Successful leaders concentrate on their ability to communicate effectively, which includes listening, trust, honesty, and vision.

➤ Leadership will require learning agility—asking insightful questions, accepting feedback, learning from mistakes.

Empty your mind of clutter, maintain an inner peace. Ten thousand things move around you. In detachment, perceive the cycles.

—Lao-tzu, the *Tao Te Ching*

DETACHMENT

Every leader must be able to detach from the immediate tactical mission and understand how it fits into strategic goals.
—Willink and Babin, *Extreme Ownership, How US Navy SEALs Lead and Win*

Detach: disengage; disconnect

Do leaders feel trampled by the speed of life, business, technology, and more in this world of accelerating complexity? Are we all living in an "age of speed," as author Vincent Poscente believes?

Perhaps the big question in this daily acceleration of complexity and chaos is, how do we capture and tame speed to our advantage? How can we find some measure of balance and reduced stress in such a volatile world? How can we put passion and more personal time into our work? How do we create more opportunities with purpose, become more open to ways to free ourselves of informational clutter, and drag that ultimately weakens our potential as leaders and human beings?

The questions for leaders come easily, the solutions, sometimes not so much. However, *detachment* offers a start.

Remove Yourself

This may, at first glance, seem to be a very strange leadership attribute.

Do good leaders really disconnect?

Do serious leaders look for solitude?

Do they truly disengage from the leadership process?

They absolutely do and do so periodically, for very good reason.

Bob Johansen, in his powerful book, *Leaders Make the Future: Ten New Leadership Skills for an Uncertain World*, comments about detachment when he writes:

> Dealing with dilemmas requires an ability to sense, frame and reframe a situation. Reframing is *stepping back*, checking assumptions and considering other ways of looking at a situation to see what's really going on and what *could* be going on.

Bold and effective leadership often requires a change in outlook and perspective. That change can begin with a focus on personal awareness and feedback about the present, which is difficult to see when your world is moving at warp speed. This will require a pause, a time for reflection, a slow-down pace to ultimately scale up to approach your desired business target(s).

Self-awareness is often cited as one of the must-haves for leadership competency. Its critical to understand your strengths and weaknesses. The Center for Creative Leadership breaks this down into four parts—wisdom, brand, reputation, and identity—all key components for leadership success in a chaotic world.

Leaders today will no doubt begin to appreciate the deeper aspects of an accelerating pace in both their personal and business orbits. With speed comes more life, more challenges, more excitement, and more significance. The challenge is to thrive, not just survive, and this demands that leaders understand their purpose, are open to new pathways, and free themselves from the clutter that can retard potential. In detachment, leaders will enhance their self-awareness and offer needed time to reset influence and review and or change desired goals.

In their 2019 book titled *Ichigo Ichie, The Art of Making the Most of Every Moment, the Japanese Way*, authors Hector Garcia and Francesc Miralles write:

> Even if what appears on your inner screen is an aberration, your attitude should be neutral, lest you stray from the assumption that "You are not your thoughts." When we separate the observer from the observed in this metacognition (ability to regulate one's own thinking and awareness) exercise, we manage to detach ourselves from our mind at the same time we observe its processes. This helps us reach a state of calm.

Don't hesitate to take a time out, get a better view of the situation at hand by removing yourself from the action, maybe you'll see things a little differently, with more clarity and direction.

Break in the Action

Stepping back periodically is, without question, linked to necessary introspection, vital self-awareness focus, and a quick and simple time to evaluate your leadership. From an article in the May 2019 edition of *SmartBrief on Leadership*, this time could be used to further evaluate your leadership by asking the following questions:

> ➤ Are people motivated to follow you?

> ➤ Do people seek your perspective or insights?

> ➤ How open are you to different perspectives on tough issues?

> ➤ What feedback causes you to become defensive?

> ➤ Why do you take certain situations personally?

> ➤ How does your communication style affect others?

> ➤ How does your mood affect the decision making of others?

> ➤ Do people view you as negative/cynical or positive/passionate?

> ➤ What characteristics of others bother you the most? (helps you develop emotional intelligence)

> ➤ Do I give others the benefit of the doubt, or do I make negative assumptions or judgments of others?

These are leadership-building questions that should be periodically revisited by taking some time to detach from your sphere of daily chaos. That daily chaos can certainly be overwhelming as the demands on leaders to keep pace with the alarming rate of business movement actually requires an increase in effectiveness at a pace faster than the world around them.

How complicated can achieving dynamic leadership be in a chaotic world? Why the need for periodic detachment to improve leadership skills and ability? Words like speed, accelerating, complexity, confusing, ambiguity, disruption, and volatility surface frequently. Navy SEALs and authors of *Extreme Ownership* Jocko Willink and Leif Babin offer the following order of events for an effective leader on any problem-packed day:

➤ Evaluate the highest priority problem.

➤ Lay out in simple, clear, and concise terms the highest priority effort for your team.

➤ Develop and determine a solution, seek input from key leaders, and from the team where possible.

➤ Direct the execution of that solution, focusing all efforts and resources toward this priority task.

➤ Move on to the next highest priority problem. Repeat.

➤ When priorities shift within the team, pass situational awareness both up and down the chain.

➤ Don't let the focus on one priority cause target fixation. Maintain the ability to see other problems developing, and rapidly shift as needed.

To function at their most effective level of leadership to tackle the above agenda, Willink and Babin outline the following leadership dichotomies and areas of needed focus:

- ➢ Confident but not cocky

- ➢ Courageous but not foolhardy

- ➢ Competitive but a gracious loser

- ➢ Attentive to details but not obsessed by them

- ➢ Strong but have endurance

- ➢ A leader and a follower

- ➢ Humble not passive

- ➢ Aggressive not overbearing

- ➢ Quiet not silent

- ➢ Calm but not robotic, logical but not devoid of emotions

Becoming detached periodically is integral to achieving balance, focusing on priorities, reassessing goals, designing a different pathway for team success and additional needed introspection for continued leadership effectiveness.

You might find it helpful to consider and absorb the following ancient wisdom:

The best leader does not use force.
The best warrior does not act in anger.
The best officer does not fight petty battles.
The best managers seek to understand their people.

This is the practice of detachment
Which brings the power to lead others
And is the highest lesson under heaven.
—Lao-tzu, *Tao Te Ching*

Making a Difference: Clarkston, Georgia

Heval Kelli, a Syrian refugee, recites his story moving to a small town in Georgia.

> Two days after we arrived, we were terrified. And then all these people arrived at our door with food, wanting to help us learn English. You know, we thought they were the CIA or something, all these white Americans knocking on our door. They didn't look at all like us. But they changed our lives. ("They" were members of Clarkston's All Saints Episcopal Church.)

Clarkston, Georgia, a working-class town of 13,000, sometimes called the Ellis Island of the South, is a small town that has taken in 40,000 refugees over the past twenty-five years. At one time the local high school had students from more than fifty countries, such as the Republic of Congo, Ethiopia, Somalia, Vietnam, Sudan, Syria, Liberia, and Bhutan. A low-priced housing market and easy transportation make it a great starter city for refugees. Their measure of success is when they accumulate enough money and education to move to Atlanta, one hour away, to continue in a chosen field of education, work, and career.

Clarkston's refugee population is key to the town's sense of identity, a compassionate and working town, a welcoming place for anyone to live regardless of ethnic origin. Regaining a sense of place is a priority for the community. One native Clarkston resident says:

> In Clarkston there's a lot of ethnic groups that were at odds with each other before and are now neighbors. You watch them learn how to love each other. I think refugees have a lot to teach Americans about forgiveness.

Is tiny Clarkston, Georgia making a difference?

Leadership lessons learned: compassion, winning attitude, perseverance, teamwork.

Detachment Key Points

➤ **"Remove" yourself every now and then.**

➤ **Practice looking inside from the outside.**

➤ **Reflect on what it means to have balance in your life.**

➤ **Take a few minutes of time out every day, think about what's going on today, tomorrow, and next week—how can you impact?**

➤ **Avoid becoming so busy you lose sight of what's really important.**

> ➤ During your periods of detachment, focus on how you can better interact with others to make good things happen.

Leadership Insights

> ➤ Leadership effectiveness is a primary contributor to business performance.

> ➤ Leadership teams must work on the quality of their engagement.

> ➤ In a chaotic world, leaders must learn how to attack dilemmas and delegate problems to others.

> ➤ Leaders are expected to set vision, capture people's imagination, provide inspiration, and instill a culture of employee value and appreciation.

Persistent gender bias too often disrupts the learning process at the heart of becoming a leader.
—Herminia Ibarra, INSEAD
—Robin Ely, Harvard Business School
—Deborah Kolb, Simmons School of Management

➤ Parisa Tabriz, Senior director of engineering for
  Chrome, Google

➤ Liz Meyerdirk, Global head of business development,
  Uber Eats

➤ Marisa Bartning, Director of marketing, Bubly, PepsiCo

➤ Laura Kilman, Senior flavor scientist, Impossible Foods

And in 2021 the following female executives, over the age of
fifty, assumed their new CEO roles:

➤ Rosalind Brewer, CEO of Walgreens Pharmacy

➤ Karen Lynch, CEO of CVS Pharmacy

➤ Carol Tome, CEO of UPS

➤ Jane Fraser, CEO of Citigroup Bank

These women, and many others, are changing the world of
business. They are smart, risk takers, bold, courageous, curious,
ask *big* questions, and find ways to tackle the myriad of dilemmas
in our chaotic world. They embrace the choice to either survive
or thrive and that's exactly what serious leaders do. And they are
definitely embracing the chaos!

What are the leadership barriers facing women today? What
are the particular female leadership attributes that separate them
from men? What does the research say about how women should
navigate the business world for optimal success?

Women often find themselves in a catch-22 situation—they must be strong and independent without being "bossy." Men become bosses; women become bossy. Yes, it's still largely a "bro culture." Often times its modesty that undermines female advancement. When women exert strength and vision, they may be termed bossy. The resulting stress in coping with female stereotypes can undermine female performance. Women may feel that their advancement and success was simply "lucky." Research reveals that there are multiple and measurable double standards impeding women's success while similarly advancing men.

Andrea Jung, former CEO of Avon Cosmetics and current President and CEO of Grameen America, a nonprofit microfinance organization, once said, "I was often the only woman or Asian sitting around a table of senior executives. I experienced plenty of meetings outside my organization with large groups of executives, where people assumed that I couldn't be the boss, even though I was."

Research by the Center for Creative Leadership in North Carolina is telling us that women are mentored more often than men, but that these mentorships are producing fewer promotions and are less likely to be provided by a senior executive. And women are less likely to have a sponsor, someone who introduces them to the "right" people and uses their influence to protect them from company politics.

In 2018, a wide-ranging Pew Research Center report found that of twelve leadership traits desired for business leaders, women scored better than men on all but three—risk taking, being persuasive and making profitable deals.

Dr. Birute Regine, the author of *Iron Butterflies: Women Transforming Themselves and the World*, contrasts female and male leadership skills as follows:

Feminine attributes—inclusion, relational intelligence, deep listening, empathy, intuition, big picture thinking, finding common ground, bridge building

Masculine attributes—being independent, strategic, linear, decisive, goal oriented, Commando style of leadership

Dr. Regine notes that, historically, these male attributes have been rewarded more by society. This makes sense, since males have long dominated the business world. But what we know in 2021 is that some combination of both feminine and masculine attributes is proving to lead to a high performing profile of big impact leaders. And perhaps most importantly, in the chaotic world of globalization, women are proving to be more transformational versus transactional. Men go for the deal. Women focus on a bigger picture down the road.

Transactional leadership drives a focus on setting direction, keeping promises, executing efficiently, and producing desired results. Transformational leadership has an eye on setting a vision that captures imagination, engaging employees with meaningful work and setting the tone for the way people are valued at work.

Cindy Adams, writing in *Women in Leadership*, refers to a recently developed 360 Degree Leadership Circle Profile model that is the only deep assessment that measures two primary leadership domains—creative competencies and reactive tendencies. She reports that current research validates that today's women leaders are significantly outperforming male leaders in almost every leadership competency category. Where do female leaders excel?

> ➤ Their teams and organizations perform with necessary agility.

> ➤ They manage complexity.

> ➤ They create supporting conditions for significant employee engagement.

> ➤ They lead with less hierarchy and bureaucracy.

> ➤ They realize that caring, empathy, kindness, and decency are valuable attributes.

And yet, women continue to face a myriad of unique challenges in the business world. This only hinders the necessary organizational potential to create dynamic leadership to excel in today's global complexity.

What can aspirational women leaders do to maximize their chances at breaking through staid barriers in a male dominated business culture?

In a 2019 *Success Magazine* article, "5 Ways High Achieving Women Can Break Through the Glass Ceiling," the following pathway was outlined:

One, women will need to raise their standards. You (women) will have to exhibit a level of excellence, be a high performer, work hard, and realize that results don't happen without rituals (habits).

Two, make more mistakes. Recognize that you will make mistakes and the value will come from lessons learned, so embrace the missteps and recognize the opportunities. Do not be risk-averse and focus on learning from failure because bold leaders will fail at times.

Three, know the difference between a mentor and a sponsor and get both. Mentors act as advisors and share their wisdom. Sponsors are senior level leaders who will actively advocate for you. Choose your support group carefully.

Four, leverage your professional tool box (skills, abilities, experiences). Find a way to incorporate all of your leadership attributes in all that you do. Leaders are lifelong learners.

Five, network, delegate, and collaborate. Focus on your most useful connections and relationships. Look outside your comfort zone, look outside your industry sector, and strengthen those bonds of influence.

Additional research tells us that women score very high in one key area of effective leadership, *emotional IQ.* In other words, how well do you make the meaningful connection with the people you lead? How well do you relate to team members? Emotional intelligence isn't about running a popularity contest, that's not what effective leaders do. But it is about creating a level of trust and belief, a level of respect and empathy with employees and those you lead.

At some point, and often more than once, a leader will have to deliver the tough news. It's critical that your team, your employees, and your relationships know that you have their best interests at heart, as difficult as that news may demand.

It's worth noting that there are three mindsets that lack emotional intelligence, and ones that both female and male leaders should avoid at all costs. They are:

The *victim*, the woe-is-me mentality, carrying the weight of the world and everything is really negative. These people are simply exhausting to be around, are terrific energy sappers, create bad air, and have no place in any business. Avoid and remove them quickly.

The *hero*, everything is great because they are present, couldn't make it without them, all blame is passed to others, they never make a mistake, and there is no room for empathy for this character. Again, avoid and remove them quickly.

The *villain*, the real tough guys/gals, the immortal badass, the diminishers, who invite trouble and have to appear tough and dangerous while bringing serious discomfort to others. They thrive on creating misery. You know what to do.

Women continue to exhibit a strong emotional IQ in a chaotic business world and their challenge will be to build on this extraordinary leadership attribute as they chart future leadership goals. Again, Dr. Birute Regine, founder of Iron Butterfly Power Circles, writes:

> By employing feminine skills women are redefining the use of power and the meaning of leadership. How do we create strong and positive relationships? By employing our feminine skills. Skills such as relational intelligence, emotional intelligence, inclusion and empathy serve to strengthen our relationships.

Shirley Osborne, CEO of Posh Affairs, Inc., a women's services group encompassing The Girls Education Project, offers the following advice for emerging female leaders:

> It is up to women, then, as we advance in the power of structures and economic institutions of the world, no matter how we acquire that advancement, to reach back, reach down, reach out, and embrace other women, pull them in, give them a hand up.

Without question, challenges remain for women leaders:

> So, I took medical leave for three months and went into debt immediately...these are issues that most women still face...one out of four US mothers returns to work just 10 days after giving birth. Federal law allows for 12 weeks of unpaid leave, but the fear women feel of going into debt or losing their job is a very real thing.
> —Mika Brzezinski, author of *Know Your Value: Women, Money and Getting What You're Worth*

Remember, it was two women, Johanna Sigurdaroottir and Halla Tomasdottir, largely given credit for embracing the economic chaos of the 2008 global recession and successfully pulling Iceland out of that financial debacle. They embraced the chaos successfully and enjoyed the journey!

> I'll be fierce for all of us, for our planet and all of our protected land.
> —Deb Haaland, US Representative from New Mexico and the first Native American cabinet member serving as the Interior Secretary beginning in 2021

The future for women in meaningful leadership roles is an exciting one and can't happen quickly enough.

When given opportunities to learn and lead, girls show us again and again that they will.
—Malala Yousafzai, student, cofounder of the Malala Fund, and the youngest person ever awarded the Nobel Peace Prize

Making a Difference

Reviewing Leila Janah's resume is like reading the highlights from every Nobel Prize winner to date:

➤ Daughter of Indian immigrants, growing up poor, taking on multiple jobs as a teenager babysitting and tutoring

➤ Attended the California Academy of Math and Science, won a scholarship at age seventeen from American Field Services, and went to Ghana to teach English to students in a village where many were blind

➤ Received a degree in African Development Studies from Harvard, going on to conduct field work in Mozambique, Senegal, and Rawanda

➤ Worked with Yale University and the University of Calgary on programs to incentivize the development of new drugs for neglected diseases

➤ In 2008, at the age of 26, she founded the nonprofit Samasource with a focus on employing low-income workers in India, Kenya, and Uganda to be become engaged in the new digital economy, earning a living wage where they lived

➤ Samasource went on to employ 11,000 people, working under contract from companies like Walmart, Facebook, Microsoft, Glassdoor, Getty Images, and Vulcan Capital, with a social mission to end global poverty by giving work to people in need

Some of Leila's awards and recognition include:

➤ Forbes Magazine Thirty Under Thirty "Rising Star" in 2011 at age twenty-nine

➤ Fortune Magazine "Most promising Entrepreneurs" in 2013 at age thirty-one

➤ The youngest person to receive the Heinz Award in Technology, Economy and Employment in 2014 at age thirty-two

➤ The New York Times Magazine Five Visionary Tech Entrepreneurs Who Are Changing the World in 2015 at age thirty-three

Leila Janah died in January 2020 at age 38 from epithelioid sarcoma, a rare form of cancer. To say that Leila was a high-impact, authentic, brave, and courageous leader is an understatement. Leila's idea of leadership, of making a difference, was to leave a meaningful imprint on the world.

What's your idea of meaningful leadership?

Leadership lessons learned: focus, perseverance, courage, intellect, disruption, urgency

Women Leaders Rising Key Points

- ➤ Do not back away from gender bias.

- ➤ Understand the barriers to your success, develop a plan.

- ➤ Think creatively, think differently, be bold and relentless.

- ➤ Focus on your proven leadership attributes.

- ➤ Make thoughtful networking a strategic priority.

Leadership Insights

- ➤ Leaders always listen first, ask questions next, *big* questions.

- ➤ Effective leadership demands questioning oneself, constantly.

- ➤ The best leaders have a very high emotional IQ.

➤ High-impact leaders often take the unconventional path.

➤ Kindness and empathy are *not* weak leadership attributes.

What if you gave yourself permission to
question everything you know and throw out
all the pieces that hold you back?
—Vishen Lakhiani

MOVING FORWARD

In the past, jobs were about muscles, now they're about brains, but in the future, they'll be about the heart.
—Minouche Shafik, director, London School of Economics

What's Next?

It should be very clear at this point that leadership is a personal commitment, and becoming a bold and courageous leader will be the ultimate key to both business and individual happiness and success. Will that be easy? Again, no it will not, and everyone will not go down that path. Basic human nature does not like change, and accelerating change even less. Most people will likely continue to look for safety and structure and avoid risk wherever possible.

That's not what catalytic and dynamic leadership is about.

It should also be very clear that the business world, and the world in general, continues to change at a mind-bending pace, and there's no evidence that will diminish. To meet the incoming challenges that presents will require an ability to become comfortable in areas of considerable discomfort.

Perhaps the trillion-dollar question is, as noted earlier, will you *survive* or *thrive*?

Education

How important is a formal education to a leader's success in this chaotic mix of the known and unknown? A business reporter for *Time* magazine recently wrote the following:

> Getting a college degree has long been integral to the mythic promise of American prosperity. Yet, for millions, it's become exactly that, a myth and a very expensive myth at that.

There's little question that a college/university degree doesn't carry the so-called guarantee it once did. And spending upward of $100M for a four-year bachelor's degree without a concrete action plan and known **ROI** (return on investment) makes little sense.

What *is* of paramount importance, though, is that whatever educational path is chosen, it results in a strong set of critical thinking skills, complex reasoning ability, and a lot of common sense. (To learn more about today's debate on the power, or lack of, a college education, you might find the following two books worth a read or review: *The Years That Matter Most: How College Makes or Breaks Us*, Paul Tough, 2019; and *Lower Ed: The Troubling Rise of For-Profit Colleges in the New Economy*, Tressie Cottom, PhD, 2018.)

We know that successful leaders are lifelong learners, they value immersive learning and are voracious readers, while focusing on becoming experts in their chosen career. Executive coach Larry Alton has advised, "Education and experience don't guarantee success—attitude and habits do."

The previous chapters have provided varied leadership input, research, and learned advice from a number of business and leadership experts. How to condense this wisdom into a takeaway summary has its risks—oversimplification or overboard complexity. As you, the student, the audience this book is intended for, begin to move forward into all the promise and reward you are looking for, it's worth highlighting a few leadership truths (and there are many) to hold onto. As outlined by the Center for Creative Leadership, they offer:

Communication
Effective leadership cannot impact without writing and speaking with clarity and conviction. Conveying clear vision, strategic intent, and identifying the *why* of what you do will drive your success. And always be the *big* listener and ask the *big* questions.

Influence
Effective leadership understands the power of influence and the ongoing value of establishing meaningful networks. Forming strong and strategic alliances, both within and outside of your immediate business circle, are critical to creating a clear pathway to success.

Self-Awareness
Effective leadership can only survive and thrive by a deep introspective look. Who are you? What's your purpose? Do you have a core set of values? This is absolutely critical for extended leadership effectiveness and strengthening your leadership skill set.

Learning Agility
Effective leadership, leadership that embraces immersive learning and values curiosity and wonder, demands that a leader recognize

when new skills are needed, when behaviors should change, and the high impact this can deliver.

A New Approach to Leadership

In 2019 leadership maverick Simon Sinek authored a new book, titled *The Infinite Game,* in which he suggests that many of today's business leaders are playing a sports-like game, one of winners and losers. Leaders playing a finite game see their business world like a sports team, a world with defined rules, boundaries, time-limits, and a beginning and end. They lead their business like playing a football game—there's a set start and end time, and at the game's conclusion, a winner is declared based on the most points scored. Someone wins and someone loses.

In contrast, leaders taking a deeper view of life and the world they do business in, prefer to see their world as infinite. There are no hard-and-fast rules, their business environment is both dynamic and fluid, ever-evolving, sometimes maintaining and other times creating, while their constant focus is working for business longevity.

Sinek says the finite game players wind up with a "default win-lose model," which often works for the short term, but with grave consequences longer term. This default mindset can result in annual rounds of employee layoffs and toxic work environments, only rewarding the top performers while overlooking the support teams that got them there. This finite culture often contributes to a decline in employee loyalty that results in a high level of anxiety and insecurity, elements that many employees are feeling today. It's a very short-sighted model that puts profit over people.

In Sinek's words:

Great leaders are the ones who think beyond "short term" versus "long term." They are the ones who know that it is not about the next quarter or the next election, it is about the next generation. Great leaders set up their organizations to succeed beyond their lifetimes, and when they do, the benefits—for us, for business and even for the shareholder—are extraordinary.

He goes on to say:

Because they are playing with an end point in mind, finite minded players do not like surprises and fear any kind of disruption. Things they cannot predict or control could upset their plans and increase their chances of losing. The infinite-minded player, in contrast, expects surprises, even revels in them, and is prepared to be transformed by them. They embrace the freedom of play and are open to any possibility that keeps them in the game. Instead of looking for ways to react to what has already happened, they look for ways to do something new. Instead of reacting to how new technology will challenge our business model, for example, those with infinite mindsets are better able to foresee the applications of new technology...As for us, those who choose to embrace an infinite mindset, our journey is one that will lead us to feel inspired every morning, safe when we are at work and fulfilled at the end of each day. And when it is our time to leave the game, we will look back at our lives and our careers and say, "I lived a life worth living." And more important, when imagining what the future holds, we will see how many people we've inspired to carry on the journey without us.

Sinek's insights on leadership effectiveness in today's chaotic economy have serious implications for the leadership path you choose to follow. It challenges many of the leadership norms that continue today, while opening a new way of thinking for meaningful change and high-impact success. Infinite game or finite game, your choice.

Leadership Continues to Requires a New Mindset

If you're not familiar with the term *growth mindset*, you should listen to what Stanford University's Professor of Psychology, Carol Dweck writes:

> Individuals who believe their talents can be developed (through hard work, good strategies, and input from others) have a *growth mindset*. They tend to achieve more than those with a more *fixed mindset* (those who believe their talents are innate gifts). This is because they worry less about looking smart and they put more energy into learning. When entire companies embrace a growth mindset, their employees report feeling far more empowered and committed...In contrast, people at primarily fixed-mindset companies report more of only one thing: cheating and deception among employees, presumably to gain an advantage in the talent race.

Professor Dweck goes on to tell us that it's not easy to acquire a growth mindset, given that most of us have built-in fixed-mindset triggers. Life and work challenges, criticism, failure, and faring poorly when compared to others, are a few of these triggers.

To overcome these fixed-mindset obstacles will require hard work and a realization that serious and effective leadership always requires a continuing path of self-reflection and immersive learning. Incorporating a growth mindset along your leadership journey will pay big dividends.

Worth Remembering

Once again, leadership is a matter of choice. Leadership is a mindset, a soulset, a heartset. Leaders are not born, there is no leadership gene.

Personal growth advisor, computer engineer, and CEO of Mindvalley, Vishen Lakhiani offers yet another leadership perspective in his recent book, *The Code of the Extraordinary Mind*. Challenging us to totally rethink how we go about our daily lives, often constrained by our narrowly defined assumptions about our more immediate surroundings and the rules we play by, Lakhiani outlines ten unconventional laws to redefine what a successful life can look like. Offering unique insights into defining the real goals that serious leaders set to achieve success and happiness, our methods of thinking to achieve "daily bliss," how we become "fear proof," and how we choose to "upgrade our beliefs," Lakhiani's provocative book should be a thoughtful read for those leaders about to tackle the chaos that awaits them.

Again, the key question is, do you want to survive or thrive?

Don't forget, much of leadership is *common sense*, but not *common practice* today. There is an alarming dearth of leadership and you will find a crisis in leadership in almost every sector of society you care to examine—health care, professional sports, politics, Fortune 500 business, religion, public education, and more. You can change that. You need to change that. You must change that.

Let me offer the following four challenges to guide you on your leadership journey.

First, be a magician, do the *unexpected*, do one thing every day that scares you.

Second, be *disruptive*, in a good way, take risks, break barriers, create needed change.

Third, be unreasonable thinkers, do the extraordinary, *never* settle for mediocrity.

Fourth, push the limits, discover, dream *big*, and understand that perhaps more often than not, the limits will push back.

And Dr. Brené Brown's leadership insights offer the following advice:

> As daring leaders, we have to stay curious about our own blind spots and how to pull those issues into view, and we need to commit to helping the people we serve find their blind spots in a way that's safe and supportive.

Keep focused on doing the right thing, not just doing things right, embrace the chaos and at the end of your career, take Robin Sharma's advice and ask yourself two *big* questions:

➢ What kind of a leader was I?

➢ How many people did I help?

What is the fruit of these teachings? Only the most beautiful and proper harvest of the truly educated—tranquility, fearlessness, and freedom. We should not trust the masses who say only the free can be educated, but rather the lovers of wisdom who say that only the educated are free.

—Epictetus, Greek Stoic philosopher, 50–135 AD

QUESTIONS FOR LEADERS IN TOUGH TIMES

> ➤ How do you intend to lead in times of disruption and uncertainty?

> ➤ How do you intend to lead when things around you are breaking down?

> ➤ Will you go where others will not go?

> ➤ Are you comfortable and effective in areas of extreme discomfort?

> ➤ How will you handle fear-based attitudes?

> ➤ How do you relate to people in times of confusion, volatility, complexity, and chaos?

> ➤ How do you intend to communicate the tough news?

> ➤ Do you know that people look for and expect relevance and strong emotional IQ from their leaders in times of extreme uncertainty?

> ➤ Have you been focused on running a popularity contest or building meaningful relationships?

➤ Can your team trust you in challenging times?

➤ Are you resilient? Do you know the value of perseverance?

➤ Are you humble, compassionate, and empathetic amid the chaos?

➤ Are you transformational, a big picture thinker, in a world of never-ending distractions?

➤ Are you grateful, and do you value your team and find time to acknowledge their work?

A LEADERSHIP LESSON FROM SUSAN CAGLE

It was 2007 and young Susan Cagle, a twenty-one-year old African American, had just hit the big time. She made an appearance on the Oprah Winfrey show. Nothing could have been further from her scope of reality only a few years prior.

Susan was raised in a cult, a very restrictive, controlling, and stifling environment for a child. "We had to do everything they told us to do," she says. "We were only allowed to read the Bible and materials written by the organization."

After spending years feeling like a prisoner and yearning for some measure of freedom, Susan escaped and began a life of her own. She was a mere teenager.

"It was like, 'Oh my gosh, I've got these feelings inside me I've always felt, a hunger for knowledge, for the world, and I was told it was wrong,'" she says. "Once I started reading, it was like, 'Wow, I need to get out of this.'"

Susan made her way to New York City and took her love of music to the streets. You see, she had a *passion* for music and wanted to be a singer-songwriter. She spent the next several years developing her talent in the subway system of NYC, giving impromptu performances to whoever might listen. She surprised and delighted subway commuters with her soulful voice and guitar play:

Basically, the subway allowed me to connect with people. In the subways I wasn't alone.

I realized, looking around at all the people rushing by me, that everybody has their own story. It made me realize that, wow, I don't have to use my background as an excuse to not do anything with my life.

For years Susan played for anyone who would listen, and then fate stepped in. Music producer Jay Levine caught Susan's act in the subway, recognized her talent, was impressed with her passion for music, and soon they began writing songs together.

One of Susan's signature songs was titled "Dear Oprah," and when Oprah heard it for the first time, she just had to meet Susan in person. The song had begun as a letter Susan wrote to Oprah at age seventeen, but never sent.

"Your story inspired me, your background, how you were brought up. You're a self-made person," she told Oprah. "It was really just me pouring out my heart in my diary to you."

Leadership lessons learned: perseverance, focus, passion, attitude, bravery

A LEADERSHIP LESSON FROM CHIEF JOSEPH

Hin-mah-too-yah-lat-kekt, English name Chief Joseph, was chief of the Nez Perce, a Native American tribe of the Wallowa Valley in Northwest Oregon in the late nineteenth century. Known for his compassionate leadership in the face of unrelenting migration by white settlers in the 1870s, the following passage, in his words, is a leadership example that transcends generation and ethnicity.

> I have heard talk and talk, but nothing is done. Good words do not last long unless they amount to something. Words do not pay for my dead people. They do not pay for my country, now overrun with white men. They do not protect my father's grave. They do not pay for all my horses and cattle. Good words will not give me back my children. Good words will not make good the promise of your war chief General Miles. Good words will not give my people good health and stop them from dying. Good words will not get my people a home where they can live in peace and take care of themselves.

> I am tired of talk that comes to nothing. It makes my heart sick when I remember all the good words and all the broken promises. There has been too

much talking by men who had no right to talk. Too many misrepresentations have been made, too many misunderstandings have come up between the white men about the Indians.

If the white man wants to live in peace with the Indian, he can live in peace. There need be no trouble. Treat all men alike. Give them the same law. Give them an even chance to live and grow. All men were made by the same Great Spirit Chief. They are all brothers. The earth is the mother of all people, and all people should have equal rights upon it.

You might as well expect the rivers to run backward as that any man who was born a free man should be contented when penned up and denied liberty to go where he pleases. If you tie a horse to a stake, do you expect he will grow fat? If you pen an Indian up on a small spot of earth and compel him to stay there, he will not be contented, nor will he grow and prosper. I have asked some of the great white chiefs where they get their authority to say to the Indian that he shall stay in one place while he sees white men going where they please. They cannot tell me.

I only ask of the government to be treated as all other men are treated. If I cannot go to my own home, let me have a home in some country where my people will not die so fast.

When I think of our condition, my heart is heavy. I see men of my race treated as outlaws and driven from country to country or shot down like animals.

I know that my race must change. We cannot hold our own with white men as we are. We ask only an even chance to live as other men live. We ask to be recognized as men. We ask that the same law shall work alike on all men. If the Indian breaks the law, punish him by the law. If the white man breaks the law, punish him also.

Let me be a free man—free to travel, free to stop, free to work, free to trade where I choose, free to choose my own teachers, free to follow the religion of my fathers, free to think and talk and act for myself—and I will obey every law or submit to the penalty.

Whenever white men treat Indians as they treat each other, then we will have no more wars. We shall all be alike—brothers of one father and one mother, with one mother, with one sky above us and one country around us, and one government for all. Then the Great Spirit Chief who rules above will smile upon this land and send rain to wash out the bloody spots made by brothers' hands from the face of the earth.

For this time the Indian race is waiting and praying. I hope that no more groans of wounded men and women will ever go to the ear of the Great

Spirit Chief above and that all people may be one people.

Leadership lessons learned: passion, compassion, focus, perseverance, intellect, clarity of purpose

A LEADERSHIP LESSON FROM TARYN DAVIS

Life was good at the moment.

Twenty-two-year-old college student and newlywed bride, Taryn Davis, had a world of joy to look forward to. She had married her best friend and soul mate, Michael, an army corporal, and his deployment to Iraq would surely go by fast. Taryn and Michael were, after all, just beginning their life together and like all young married couples, the possibilities for a life of happiness seemed endless.

On May 21, 2007, Taryn met the uniformed soldier at the door and immediately heard the words, "We regret to inform you…" She knew in that horrifyingly I'm-going-numb moment that her life would never be the same. Her one and only true love, Michael, had been killed by roadside bombs in Iraq, only ninety minutes after they had last talked.

Grief stricken, seemingly alone in her new world without Michael, Taryn received the six black boxes with Michael's belongings. As she opened each box one-by-one, not knowing exactly what was in each, she sifted through clothes, photos, letters, pictures, Michael's laptop, sheets, a pillow, and uniforms. She hoped to pick up Michael's scent, to capture one last grasp of the man she loved and would never see again. Taryn began to realize that she was yet another victim of the tragedy of war.

Or was she?

Over the next four months, Taryn began a mission to meet other war widows, to try and understand their grief as she tried to understand her own. In many ways, her new life was that of a military widow, but Taryn was determined to move away from the sorrow and loneliness, away from the darkness of losing the love of your life. She soon found inspiration in the lives of other women in her same situation, all looking for answers, all seeking help and support to cope with an unimaginable tragedy.

Taryn soon realized that her love for Michael was eternal, that the lessons and things her husband had said still ran through her veins and mostly, she realized that she was not alone. Four months after Michael died, Taryn started a nonprofit foundation for war widows, creating a website that offered a forum for online support, advice, and inspiration. In no time Taryn had reached almost 1,000 women of all ages, all having lost a husband, a son, a grandson, a friend.

Taryn did what all leaders do, she picked herself up, she looked at adversity eye-to-eye, and she decided she would be the winner, not the loser. She embraced the concept of *servant leadership*, quietly but effectively reaching out to others, asking how she might help them, searching for ways to make a positive impact on others.

Taryn's foundation, the American Widow Project (www.americanwidowproject.org), is active today and serves as an amazing example of what choosing a path of leadership can do to positively impact thousands of people. Taryn created meaningful change and in doing so, was able to touch many, many lives.

Taryn Davis epitomizes winning attitude, compassion, perseverance, focus, passion, balance, and being a little unreasonable in the face of so much tragedy and adversity.

You can learn much from Taryn Davis. Visit her website, send her an email, and copy her winning attitude in all that you do.

Leadership lessons learned: perseverance, compassion, focus, teamwork, attitude

A WORD ABOUT NARCISSISM

In particular, we recommend that companies should avoid putting highly narcissistic members in the most critical team roles.
—"How Narcissism Affects Group Performance,"
Harvard Business Review, May–June 2020

This is a hard word to spell and tricky to pronounce, but it's a real word with real meaning, and it's worth a quick mention in today's society, particularly when we talk about what it takes to be an effective leader.

The word comes to us from Greek mythology. Narcissus was a mythological hero who was exceptionally attractive, so much so that he came to disdain all others in the belief that he was the most attractive person on earth. Upon seeing his reflection in a pool of water and not realizing that it was his own, he became so absorbed with the reflection's beauty that he could not break away from the pool's edge. There he died.

Today we use the word to define a condition that represents an *inflated view of self-worth*, sometimes described as self-love and or having an excessive interest in one's comfort or appearance. It basically describes someone who cares little about the genuine feelings of others and is singularly focused on his or herself. It goes beyond arrogance and conceit.

The problem we see in today's society is that an increasing number of people, sometimes beginning in young adulthood and continuing with people well into their thirties and forties, are acting out as if they are *the* only being of any importance. It's the all-about-me syndrome.

The cultural evolution of the increase in narcissistic behavior within our society is beyond the scope of this book. Having said that, let me offer a very brief insight into this potentially very damaging behavior trait.

Without question, there has been an increasing trend over the past thirty years for parents to foster a high level of self-esteem in their children. The drive is to nurture feelings of self-confidence, feelings of "you're special," feelings of "you're a winner," and increased feelings of self-worth. The danger has been that many parents now carry this war cry for success to an extreme. Witness plugging baby up to "educational" CDs at age one, having in-home tutors at age three, "pulling strings" to get junior into the city's most prestigious private school, and more. Many parents are known for doing Suzi's homework throughout her school years and, yes, even into college. In 2018–19 some very wealthy Hollywood parents were found to have bribed select colleges and universities to accept their less than qualified children. One payment was found to be $6.5 million.

This has led to our country's very blurred distinction between self-worth and narcissism. There appears to be an increasing acceptance of doing whatever it takes to get ahead. It's a competitive world, right?

We all know how competitive our world has become. Grades, athletics, jobs, family, college, career planning, it can be all-consuming, as we have already discussed.

What you should know about leadership and narcissism is that you don't need to be the latter to effectively be the former.

Studies have shown that the most successful and effective leaders are humble, avoid the limelight, work behind the scenes, work through people (teamwork), readily give credit to others, continually look for better ways to get things done, and generally are always engaged in self-improvement. Successful leaders tend to work quietly and are not self-serving media hogs. Yes, there are exceptions, but they are not the rule. Authentic leaders are not narcissistic in their behavior.

I want to make it clear that the leadership principles covered in this book in no way cross over into the realm of narcissism. Having a *winning attitude* is not about arrogance and conceit, not about self-love and is not narcissistic behavior. Embracing a *positive outlook* is not narcissistic behavior. Feeling *self-confident*, showing *passion* for your interests, and setting lofty *goals* is not narcissistic behavior. Learning how to navigate and direct *creative disruption* in our chaotic world is not narcissistic behavior.

What *is* narcissistic behavior is a feeling that you are better than everyone else, that you are, for some reason, "entitled" to a certain lifestyle, that the world revolves around you, and that you have no feeling for the values of anyone else. Narcissists love to be know-it-alls. Clinical studies have shown that they are so smart they even know things that don't actually exist.

This incessant feeling of entitlement is said to be a serious disorder in our society. However, embracing the leadership characteristics and behaviors discussed in this book in no way puts you into the realm of narcissistic behavior. Remember what we said about achieving *balance* in life? Do this and there's no need for the word narcissism in your active vocabulary.

Narcissus died looking at his reflection. Serious leaders, you, have better things to do.

FOR THOUGHT

- ➤ Leaders are often culture shifters, change makers, and disrupters.

- ➤ Leaders do what others will not do.

- ➤ Leaders do what is sometimes uncomfortable.

- ➤ Leaders are not concerned about titles and the C-Suite corner office.

- ➤ Leaders do what is sometimes unpopular, and they exhibit bravery and courage.

- ➤ Leaders are always dreaming.

- ➤ Leaders are always learning.

- ➤ Leaders are always reading.

- ➤ Leaders don't pay a lot of attention to critics.

- ➤ Leaders are relevant and have a big emotional IQ.

- ➤ Leaders look to be really good at what they do, *really* good.

- ➤ Leaders show great patience and focus.

- ➤ Leaders always look for opportunity in crisis.

- ➤ Leaders spend time with "misfits"—they know the value of thinking differently.

- ➤ Leaders look for solitude frequently—they are good at reflecting on past actions.

- ➤ Leaders do not avoid areas of life that may frighten others.

- ➤ Leaders know they will grow as they move closer to areas of discomfort.

- ➤ Leaders are givers, not takers.

- ➤ Leaders know that vague plans give vague results.

- ➤ Leaders aren't in reactive mode.

- ➤ Leaders know how to deliver the tough news in times of distress.

- ➤ Leaders have *fun*!

IT'S DEFINITELY NOT WHAT WE JUST TALKED ABOUT

Here is one big alternative to all that we have just covered in the big-bang, creative-disrupting chaos of leadership learnings.

From *I'm Done With Leadership, Here's a Better Idea*, Madrid-based leadership coach Pino Gallagher argues that leadership is little more than a race to the top. In her fifteen years of leadership focus and writings, she offers the following:

> Basically, the science of leadership is one huge, global, mumbo-jumbo of obvious facts and myths that nobody lives up to. There are too many examples of leaders in today's society who are incomplete, partial, and too often, shamelessly corrupt. It seems as if the qualities and habits we coaches and professors speak about escape many of today's leaders.

She goes on to emphasize the "clearly defined goal" is nothing more than "getting to the top." She feels this sprint to the top is rigged in favor of those with money, political influence, personal connections, and so forth. Basically, it's a top 1 percent of society who has the inside track to big leadership.

I would aggressively challenge Ms. Gallagher that her theory is seriously flawed. While history is full of her examples, and money and connections can make certain things happen for a fortunate few (or many), a closer look reveals a very different picture. This book profiles a number of individuals who have achieved serious leadership results without birth privilege, and the world is full of like people, those overcoming extreme challenges and difficulties to accomplish amazing things as a leader, big money and royal birth certificate not required. For the most part, we don't hear these hidden stories; rather, the media focus seems to be on what grabs a headline and sells print.

It's also interesting to read that Ms. Gallagher says that we should focus on our personal growth, and says that since personal growth has no explicit target or result, we would eventually have the attributes that we consider ideal for effective leadership—generosity, integrity, self-sacrifice, an absence of selfishness or egotistic behavior, wisdom, simplicity, inspirational speech, and great emotional grounding in the face of adversity.

The catch here is that personal growth is open to anyone's interpretation and therefore can't be objectively validated as a guaranteed path to successful leadership.

I do think Ms. Gallagher offers a very serious observation, though. There are a ton of so-called leaders in today's society that are anything but that. Corrupt, egotistical, arrogant, condescending, aloof, small-minded, destructive, and so forth. But they are few in number compared to average people who continue to commit to a life of extraordinary leadership and lead with humility, grace, kindness, courage, curiosity, strength, motivation, intellect, purpose, and service.

The more I study and reflect on my own leadership journey, I'm not sure that there actually is real science to leadership. The definition of leadership is wide open and while this book presents an outline of important leadership attributes, characteristics, and behaviors, the end results are always dependent on the individual's actions and accomplishments. As emphasized earlier, two key questions should surface during and at the end of a leader's career:

First, how good a leader am I/was I?

Second, how many people am I helping / did I help along the way?

I prefer to think that there are, and will be, infinitely more people asking the above two questions than those stepping on others only to count their money and prestige.

As you think about your own path to daring leadership...choose courage over comfort. Choose whole hearts over armor. And choose the great adventure of being brave and afraid. At the exact same time.

—Dr. Brené Brown, *Daring to Lead*

You are a light. You are the light. Never let anyone—any person or any force—dampen, dim or diminish your light. Study the path of others to make your way easier and more abundant.
  —John Lewis, US House of Representatives, Civil Rights Leader 1940–2020

A WORD TO PARENTS

If curiosity has led you to read this book, and I certainly hope that has occurred, then obviously, this is a book written for young students—primarily middle and high school—and collectively, young adults in general.

Now, as both a parent and a new grandparent, I feel my leadership message, one that I have given immediate purpose and importance toward, would be incomplete without a concise and relevant word to you, the parents and leaders of a new generation of game changers, your children, the gifted ones who will give us clarity in a complex and chaotic world.

The following brief excerpt from Clayton Christensen's insightful book, *How Will You Measure Your Life?*, is, in my estimation, beyond profound. Please read and reread. It's the simplest of meaning, yet also the deepest of thought as you, we, confront our biggest life-challenge.

> The challenges your children face serve an important purpose: they will help them hone and develop the capabilities necessary to succeed throughout their lives. Coping with a difficult teacher, failing at a sport, learning to navigate the complex social structure of cliques in school—all those things become "courses" in the school of experience. We

know that people who fail in their jobs often do so not because they are inherently incapable of succeeding, but because their experiences have not prepared them for the challenges of that job—in other words, they've taken the wrong "courses."

The natural tendency of many parents is to focus entirely on building your child's resume: good grades, sports successes, and so on. It would be a mistake, however, to neglect the courses your children need to equip them for the future. Once you have that figured out, work backward: find the right experiences to help them build the skills they'll need to succeed. It's one of the greatest gifts you can give them.

So be well, lead your children to the happiness and success they're so very capable and deserving of. It won't be easy, but remember, we don't plan to fail, we just fail to plan.

ACKNOWLEDGMENTS

Books are never solo efforts, and this one is no exception.

There have been countless people, all leaders in some capacity, who have sparked my interest in the subject over the years. Some have been good leaders, some have been not so good, and a rare few have been game changers. To all of these journeymen and women, you have my eternal gratitude for lessons learned.

To friends Charlotte Amos, Carol Widmeyer, Jack Dillard, Andrea Galioto-Evans, Pat Meisky, Michaux Crocker, Michelle Carter, Ed Price, Ashby Cook, Georgiana Wellford, Butch Estes, LaTinda Moore and Kayla Slater, my most sincere thanks for your critique, your candor, your time and intelligence. Your days are busy and the demands on your time are heavy, but you did for me what all strong leaders do—you found a way to work on yet another objective. You guys are the best.

Extraordinary things happen when big-time leaders get involved with a project. Tom Booker and Natalie Hutchinson of the Cannon School in Concord, NC, and Charlotte Country Day School in Charlotte, NC, set the pace for a category-creating school leadership development program using the first edition on its initial release in 2012. Their intellect and foresight have changed young lives in an instant.

Like programs followed at select schools in both North and South Carolina in addition to the unexpected—Ronald McDonald

House Charities of NE Ohio, Chamber of Commerce leadership team, ER physician and staff, US Army recruiting team, YMCA staff, a Prisons Educational Services Division working with inmates ages thirteen to twenty-one, and many others. Each of these forward-thinking organizations have my sincere appreciation for doing what serious leaders do—create meaningful change in the most challenging times.

I want to issue a special word of thanks and gratitude to the Newcomers School in Greensboro, North Carolina. A unique school whose students are all either immigrants or refugees, they chose the previous edition (2013) of this book to work with their selected high school student leadership team. These student leaders in turn model leadership success to the younger grades by embracing the key attributes and behaviors found in that book. I am confident they will find this new edition a strong follow-up and their leadership impact will no doubt continue.

To Sally, much thanks for letting me break the bank on one leadership book after another over the years. We all make sacrifices in life, big and small, but yours has been larger than planned. Thank you for your support, understanding, and putting up with some "creative disruption."

And to our children—Will, Sarah, and Chuck—you are important players in the genesis of this edition. Continuing to see your awesome leadership potential, I know the struggles and the triumphs can have serious meaning for others. You guys are my favorite leaders. Carry On.

ABOUT THE AUTHOR

Father, business owner, mountain climber, US triathlon 70.3 Ironman World Team selection, and community volunteer Bill McKenzie believes there is an unmistakable common denominator to both the educational and corporate chaos we continue to witness. Spending years analyzing and reflecting on why so many companies grind away in mediocrity while bright and energetic young people struggle to make a meaningful impact, he believes there is a lack of fundamental leadership skills that were never learned and embraced at an early age, therefore never carried forward into one's personal and business life. A college athlete and graduate of Davidson College, he holds an MA degree with honors from the University of North Carolina. This is his third book since 2012 on leadership for students and young adults, incorporating new research and outlining some of the most critical leadership attributes and behaviors necessary to succeed in today's chaotic and disruptive world.

SELECT MUST READS

1. *Leading Women: 20 Influential Women Share Their Secrets to Leadership, Business and Life* (2015) by Nancy O'Reilly

2. *The Tao of Pooh* (1982) by Benjamin Hoff

3. *The Leader Who Had No Title* (2010) by Robin Sharma

4. *Leaders Make the Future* (2012) by Bob Johansen

5. *Dare to Lead* (2018) by Brené Brown

6. *Start With WHY: How Great Leaders Inspire Everyone To Take Action* (2009) by Simon Sinek

7. *Great Leaders Have No Rules* (2019) by Kevin Kruse

8. *Multipliers* (2010) by Liz Wiseman

9. *Tribes* (2008) by Seth Godin

10. *Make Your Bed* (2017) by Admiral William H. McRaven

11. *The Art of Possibility* (2000) by Rosamund and Benjamin Zander

12. *The Lakota Way* (2001) by Joseph Marshall III

13. *Tao Te Ching, A New English Version* (1988) by Stephen Mitchell

14. *Mastering Leadership* (2016) by Robert Anderson and William Adams

15. *Fail Fast, Fail Often* (2013) by Ryan Babineaux

16. *Meditations* by Marcus Aurelius, A New Translation (2003) by Gregory Hays

17. *On The Edge* (2014) by Alison Levine

18. *The Infinite Game* (2019) by Simon Sinek

19. *Aristotle's Way* (2019) by Edith Hall

20. *Mindset, The New Psychology of Success* (2016) by Carol Dweck, PhD

21. *Pivot to the Future* (2019) by Omar Abbosh, Paul Nunes and Larry Downes

22. *Extreme Ownership: How US Navy SEALS Lead and Win* (2015) by Jocko Willink and Leif Babin

23. *Big Bang Disruption* (2014) by Larry Downes and Paul Nunes

24. *The Code of the Extraordinary Mind* (2016) by Vishen Lakhiani

25. *The Starfish and the Spider: The Unstoppable Power of Leaderless Organizations* (2009) by Ori Brafman and Rod A. Beckstrom

REFERENCES

1. *The Code of the Extraordinary Mind* (2016) by Vishen Lakhiani

2. *The Infinite Game* (2019) by Simon Sinek

3. *Aristotle's Way* (2019) by Edith Hall

4. *The Day the World Ended at Little Big Horn* (2007) by Joseph Marshall III

5. *The Lakota Way* (2001) by Joseph Marshall III

6. *Meditations,* Marcus Aurelius A New Translation (2003) by Gregory Hays

7. *Barking Up The Wrong Tree* (2017) by Eric Barker

8. *The Starfish and the Spider* (2006) by Ori Brafman and Rod Beckstrom

9. *Make Your Bed* (2017) by Admiral William H. McRaven

10. *Start With Why: How Great Leaders Inspire Everyone to Take Action* (2009) by Simon Sinek

11. *Pivot to the Future: Discovering Value and Creating Growth in a Disrupted World* (2019) by Omar Abbosh, Paul Nunes, and Larry Downes

12. *Dare to Lead: Brave Work, Tough Conversations, Whole Hearts* (2018) by Brené Brown

13. *Extreme Ownership: How U.S. Navy SEALS Lead and Win* (2015) by Jocko Willink and Leif Babin

14. *Great Leaders Have No Rules: Contrarian Leadership Principles to Transform Your Team and Business* (2019) by Kevin Kruse

15. *The Age of Speed: Learning to Thrive in a More-Faster-Now World* (2008) by Vince Poscente

16. *Big Bang Disruption: Strategy in the Age of Devastating Innovation* (2014) by Larry Downes and Paul Nunes

17. *The Dip: A Little Book That Tells You When to Quit (and When to Stick)* (2007) by Seth Godin

18. *Tribes: We Need YOU to Lead Us* (2008) by Seth Godin

19. *The Leader Who Had No Title* (2010) by Robin Sharma

20. *Leading Women: 20 Influential Women Share Their Secrets to Leadership, Business and Life* (2015) by Nancy D. O'Reilly, PSYD

21. *Leaders Make the Future: Ten New Leadership Skills for an Uncertain World* (2012) by Bob Johansen

22. *Mastering Leadership: An Integrated Framework for Breakthrough Performance and Extraordinary Business Results* (2016) by Robert J. Anderson and William A. Adams

23. *Focus: The Hidden Driver of Excellence* (2013) by Daniel Goleman

24. *Fail Fast, Fail Often: How Losing Can Help You WIN* (2013) by Ryan Babineaux, PhD and John Krumboltz, PhD

25. *Management of the Absurd: Paradoxes in Leadership* (1996) by Richard Farson

26. *Leadership Secrets of Attila the Hun* (1985) by Wess Roberts, PhD

27. *Primal Leadership: Unleashing the Power of Emotional Intelligence* (2013) by Daniel Goleman, Richard Boyatzis, and Annie McKee

28. *Drive: The Surprising Truth About What Motivates Us* (2009) by Daniel H. Pink

29. *The Power of Noticing: What the Best Leaders See* (2014) by Max H. Bazerman

30. *Patton on Leadership: Strategic Lessons for Corporate Warfare* (1999) by Alan Axelrod

31. *The Leadership Moment: Nine True Stories of Triumph and Disaster and Their Lessons for Us All* (1998) by Michael Useem

32. *The One Thing You Need to Know: About Great Managing, Great Leading, and Sustained Individual Success* (2005) by Marcus Buckingham

33. *Good To Great: Why Some Companies Make the Leap and Others Don't* (2001) by Jim Collins

34. *The 48 Laws of Power* (1998) by Robert Greene and Joost Elffers

35. *The Art of Possibility: Transforming Professional and Personal Life* (2000) by Rosamund Stone Zander and Benjamin Zander

36. *Leading with Soul: An Uncommon Journey of Spirit* (1995) by Lee G. Bolman and Terrence E. Deal

37. *The Japanese Samurai Code; Classic Strategies for Success* (2004) by Boye Lafayette De Mente

38. *The Tao of Personal Leadership* (1997) by Diane Dreher

39. *The Tao of Pooh* (1982) by Benjamin Hoff

40. *The Samurai Leader: Winning Business Battles with the Wisdom, Honor and Courage of the Samurai Code* (2005) by Bill Diffenderffer

41. *How to Become CEO: The Rules for Rising to the Top of Any Organization* (1998) by Jeffrey J. Fox

42. *Managing People Is Like Herding Cats* (1997) by Warren Bennis

43. *Machiavelli On Modern Leadership: Why Machiavelli's Iron Rules Are as Timely and Important Today as Five Centuries Ago* (1999) by Michael A. Ledeen

44. *Leadership Lessons of the Navy SEALS: Battle-Tested Strategies for Creating Successful Organizations and Inspiring Extraordinary Results* (2003) by Jeff Cannon and Lt. Cmdr. Jon Cannon

45. *John Kotter on What Leaders Really Do* (1999) by John Kotter, Professor of Leadership at the Harvard Business School

46. *Sun Tzu, The Art of War for Managers: 50 Strategic Rules* (2001) by Gerald A. Michaelson

47. *Strategy of the Dolphin: Scoring a Win in a Chaotic World* (1988) by Dudley Lynch and Paul L. Kordis

48. *On Becoming a Leader* (1994) by Warren Bennis

49. *Sun Tzu and the Art of Business: Six Strategic Principles for Managers* (1996) by Mark McNeilly

50. *The Tao of Leadership* (1985) by John Heider

51.   *The Age of Unreason* (1989) by Charles Handy

52.   *Management Challenges for the 21st Century* (1999) by Peter Drucker

53.   *If Aristotle Ran General Motors: The New Soul of Business* (1997) Tom Morris

54.   *Reinventing Leadership: Strategies to Empower the Organization* (1995) by Warren Bennis and Robert Townsend

55.   *The Way of the Warrior: Business Tactics and Techniques from History's Twelve Greatest Generals* (1997) by James Dunnigan and Daniel Masterson

56.   *The Power of Full Engagement: Managing Energy, Not Time, Is the Key to High Performance and Personal Renewal* (2003) by Jim Loehr and Tony Schwartz

57.   *The Age of Paradox* (1994) by Charles Handy

58.   *Lead with Humility: 12 Leadership Lessons from Pope Francis* (2015) by Jeffrey Krames

59.   *The Genius of Sitting Bull: 13 Heroic Strategies for Today's Business Leaders* (1993) by Emmett C. Murphy with Michael Snell

60.   *The Monk who Sold His Ferrari: A Fable about Fulfilling Your Dreams and Reaching Your Destiny* (1997) by Robin S. Sharma

61. *Hagakure: The Book of the Samurai* (2002) Yamamoto Tsunetomo, translated by William Scott Wilson

62. *Multipliers: How the Best Leaders Make Everyone Smarter* (2010) by Liz Wiseman

63. *On the Edge: The Art of High-Impact Leadership* (2014) Alison Levine

64. *Leading Change* (1996) by John P. Kotter

65. *Warrior Politics: Why Leadership Demands a Pagan Ethos* (2002) by Robert D. Kaplan

66. *The Stuff of Heroes: The Eight Universal Laws of Leadership* (1998) by William A. Cohen, PhD Major General, USAFR. RET.

67. *Black Elk Speaks* (1932, 1959, 1972, 1979) by John G. Neihardt and the University of Nebraska Press

68. *The Tao te Ching: A New English Version* (1988) by Stephen Mitchell

69. *Peace Is Every Step: The Path of Mindfullness in Everyday Life* (1991) by Thich Nhat Hanh

70. *Touching Peace: Practicing the Art of Mindful Living* (1992) by Thich Nhat Hanh

71. *Fragrant Palm Leaves: Journals 1962–1966* (1966) by Thich Nhat Hanh

72.   *The Miracle of Mindfulness* (1975) by Thich Nhat Hanh

73.   *Harvard Business Review on Breakthrough Thinking* (1999) by President and Fellows of Harvard College

74.   *Harvard Business Review on Leadership* (1998) by President and Fellows of Harvard College

75.   *Time* Magazine, November 7, 2017; August 2018; September 17, 2018; May 18, 2018; May 28, 2018

76.   *Fortune* Magazine, October 2019; August 2018; January 2019; January 2020

77.   *Forbes* Magazine, August 31, 2018; September 30, 2018

78.   *Sports Illustrated*, March 26, 2018

79.   *The Week*, December 14, 2018

80.   *Harper's* Magazine, December 2018

81.   *Real Leaders* Magazine, January 10, 2017; August 16, 2018

82.   *Iron Butterflies: Women Transforming Themselves and the World* (2010) by Birute Regine

83.   "#Gratitude" by Carol E. Quillen, President, Davidson college, *The Davidson College Journal*, Fall/Winter 2019

84. "I'm Done With 'Leadership.' Here's a Better Idea" by Pino Gallager, *Real Leaders* Magazine, 2018

85. "College Is a Racket" by Rebecca Kantar, *Bloomberg Businessweek*, March 20, 2019

86. "The Lost Generation (The Job Crisis Is Hitting Young People Especially Hard—Imperiling Their Future and the Economy)" by Peter Coy, *BusinessWeek*, October 19, 2009

87. "Focused Leaders" by Daniel Goleman, *Harvard Business Review*, December 2013

88. "How Narcissism Affects Group Performance," *Harvard Business Review*, May–June 2020

89. "Maybe Failure Isn't the Best Teacher" by Lauren Eskreis-Winkler, *Harvard Business Review*, May–June 2020

90. "The Real Leadership Lessons of Steve Jobs" by Walter Isaacson, *Harvard Business Review*, April 2012

91. "The Big Shift: How Managers Become Leaders" by Michael D. Watkins, *Harvard Business Review*, June 2102

92. "A Great Place to Work: What IDEO, BlackRock and Netflix Know about Building High-Performance Cultures," *Harvard Business Review*, January–February 2014

93. "Big Bang Disruption: A New Can of Innovator Can Wipe Out Incumbents in a Flash" by Larry Downes and Paul Nunes, *Harvard Business Review*, March 2013

94. "Emotional, Bossy, Too Nice: The Biases That Still Hold Female Leaders Back—And How to Overcome Them," *Harvard Business Review*, September 2013

95. "Manage Your Work, Manage Your Life: Zero in on What Really Matters" by Boris Groysberg and Robin Abrahams, *Harvard Business Review*, March 2014

96. "Surviving Disruption" by Maxwell Wessel and Clayton Christensen, *Harvard Business Review*, December 2012

97. "20 Ideas That Will Shape The 2020s," *Fortune Magazine*, January 2020

98. *The Book of Ichigo Ichie, The Art of Making the Most of Every Moment, the Japanese Way* (2019) by Hector Garcia and Francesc Miralles

99. *On the Shortness of Life by Seneca*, translated by Damian Stevenson (2018)

100. *The Coddling of the American Mind* (2018) by G. Lukianoff and J. Haidt

101. Economy, *Time* magazine, August 17/August 24, 2020

102. *How Will You Measure Your Life* (2012) by Clayton M. Christensen

103. *Mindset, the New Psychology of Success* (2016) by Carol Dweck, PhD

104. *Lead Yourself First, Inspiring Leadership Through Solitude* (2017), by Raymond Kethledge and Michael Irwin

CPSIA information can be obtained
at www.ICGtesting.com
Printed in the USA
JSHW050213300622
27470JS00004BA/19